MORE
Leeds
MEMORIES

The publishers would like to thank the following companies for their support in the production of this book

Main Sponsor
Armstrong Priestley

A Baldwin & Co. (Builders) Ltd

Berwin & Berwin Ltd

City Varieties Music Hall

Clariant

Evans Property Group

Gateways School

Geo. Spence and Sons Ltd

Hall & Botterill Ltd

Harold Newsome Ltd

A Harrison (Bedding) Ltd

Leeds Grand Theatre

Lowe Engineering

Opera North

Redmayne-Bentley

Sanderson Weatherall

Scattergood & Johnson

Viamaster Transport Ltd

Woodhouse Grove School

Yorkshire Fittings

First published in Great Britain by True North Books Limited
England HX3 6AE
01422 344344

ISBN 1 903204 90 9

Text, design and origination by True North Books
Printed and bound by The Amadeus Press

MORE *Leeds* MEMORIES

CONTENTS

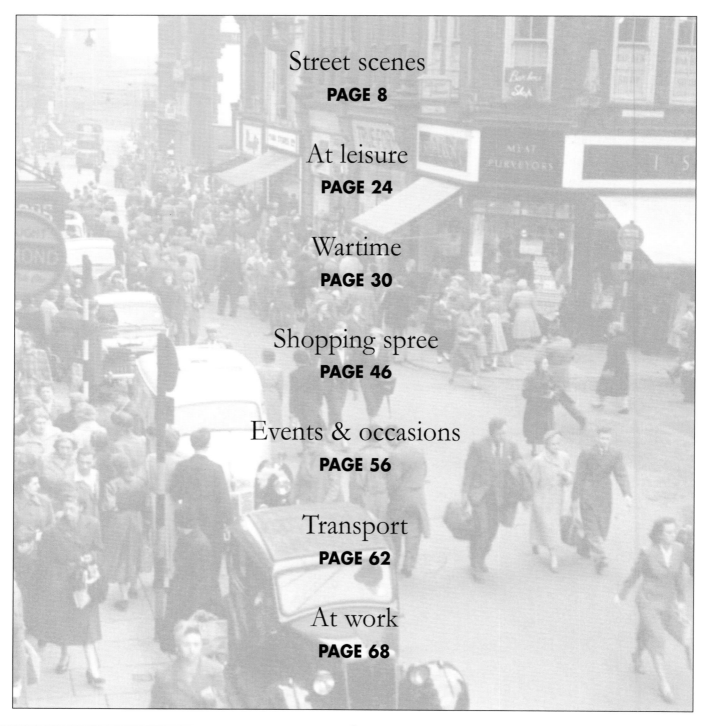

INTRODUCTION

In quiet moments we all sit back to reflect on the past. We dream of those days of yesteryear when everything seemed so much sunnier, when we were more content with life as it was. Perhaps we are fooling ourselves, but it is no sin to draw comfort from experiences through which we have lived or about which our parents told us. It does help to have a prop to help and that is where 'More Leeds Memories' will play its part. Within these pages is a wealth of nostalgia spanning the middle years of the last century. As the reader leafs through the book many half forgotten memories will come flooding back. Things that an older generation told us of will be there in black and white, firming up the mental images of a city that seemed to be locked into a time capsule out of our reach. The lovely photographs and accompanying text, variously informative, poignant and wry, help bring back to life a place that has changed so much as the years have unfolded. It is not just the buildings, skylines and thoroughfares that have altered but a whole way of life. The pace of the days when we were young or our parents were alive is brought back to mind within this nostalgic trip down memory lane. With the turning of each page will come a visit to the corner of Albion Street and Boar Lane to get granddad's deaf aid from FC Milnes, a call at the Norwich Union offices on the edge of City Square to cash in a policy or a wander along to the Fifty Shilling Tailor on Briggate for a cheap and cheerful suit. But it is not only the sights of the town that have changed. Even the vocabulary of the era that we examine in 'More Leeds Memories' has undergone a transformation. Then we spent tanners, bobs and half crowns as we did our shopping. Everything was weighed out on scales that measured in pounds and ounces without fear of shopkeepers being prosecuted by our lords and masters in government who seem to regard metrication as a god to be worshipped. We ran

up curtains by the inch, not the centimetre, and used words like 'please' and 'thank you'. 'Good morning' was a phrase used as we passed someone in the street without fear of being accused of harassment. Our children called neighbours 'uncle' or 'aunty', but now they are not spoken to because we do not even know their names. Mugging meant looking at someone's face, crack was a joke or a gap in the pavement and joyriding was a happy journey. Now we have spin in politics when once it was the prerogative of Eric Hollies, Jim Laker or Hedley Verity. But, with every hankering for the return of the old times and their values there must be some realism that it was not all days of wine and roses. There were also slum properties, areas of poverty and deprivation and the sheer horror of a world war that brought death and destruction raining down from the skies as enemy planes bombed our factories and homes.

Although this book is in no way intended to be a dry and dusty historical tome, it is still important to reflect briefly on the changes that have moulded Leeds and its inhabitants, the 'Loiners', over many centuries. The nickname for local people probably came from a corruption of Loidis or Leodis, the term in use by the eighth century for the district around the modern-day city. Others suggest that in Victorian times there were many yards and closes around Briggate whose back entrances were known as Low Ins or Loins. A third theory would have us believe that it came from a local pronunciation of 'lanes' where people used to congregate to gossip.

In Saxon times, a small village grew amid the farmland that dominated the district. Inhabitants only numbered about 200 when the Norman Conquest came and the 1086 Domesday Book had little more to say about it. Things began to alter more dramatically in subsequent years. Trade and commerce were on the increase and many new towns were being founded. In 1207, the Lord of the Manor, Maurice de Gant (Maurice Paynel), was the inspiration behind the building of a new street of housing to the west of the village. The land was divided into plots and a medieval equivalent of a population boom began. Bridge Gata, the name given to the new street, eventually became the Briggate we know today. As well as the traditional carpenters, butchers, bakers, chandlers and blacksmiths came the main local industry of wool manufacture. The material was woven, fulled and dyed and made ready for sale at the markets and fairs. Although increasing in population to about 1,000, Leeds

was still a small market town, dwarfed in importance by Wakefield, York and Beverley. The provision of fulling mills in the 14th century helped the town to expand its influence. By the end of the Tudor period, Leeds, and its woollen industry were growing rapidly. The upland areas to the west of Leeds were not self sufficient in agricultural produce and clothiers from these areas, bringing their cloth to market, needed to buy food. This was provided by farmers from the more fertile plain to the east who brought their produce to sell in the town. This meant that a thriving market developed in Leeds, and as the woollen industry grew, so did trade in other goods. Arable and industrial interests served each other well and many people moved into the area to set up in business. By now, Leeds had overtaken its neighbouring rivals in importance and the population had soared to 3,000. Later, making the Aire and Calder rivers navigable gave access to Hull and, thus, overseas markets. Opportunities for even greater wealth were enhanced when the Leeds-Liverpool Canal was completed in 1816.

By then, the industrial revolution was well under way and the Leeds skyline was undergoing great changes. Tall chimneys belching out noxious fumes, heavy machinery housed in large mills and huge warehouses dominated. During the first half of the 19th century the population more than tripled to 100,000 by the time of the 1851 census. Overcrowding and disease went hand in hand, but a major slum clearance programme towards the end of the century and major attempts to assist the lot of the poor had a large effect on the stability of the town. In 1893, Leeds was honoured by the awarding of city status.

Now it is time to venture into the world of the last century. It is over to you, the reader, to bring your imagination and memories to the pages within. Take a mental tram ride along The Headrow as you sit curled up in a horsehair armchair sucking on a stick of barley sugar or puffing away at a ciggie taken from a packet of Player's Weights, a glass of dandelion and burdock bubbling away at your side. Wind up the gramophone and put on a crackly 78 as you enjoy again the sound of Ronnie Hilton's 'No other love'. Take that baseball hat from your grandson's head and plonk a school cap firmly onto his Brylcreemed hair as you share with him the nostalgic joy that is 'More Leeds Memories'.

STREET SCENES

The mighty Royal Exchange Building dominates this prewar view across City Square. It fell foul of the demolition men's swinging ball in the mid 1960s and was replaced by an unimaginative office block. The man in the foreground sported the traditional flat cap of the northern worker, but notice how he is dressed in a suit, plus a collar and tie. Not for him the jogging bottoms, training shoes and T-shirts that we see around the city centre these days. When you went out and about in the 1930s you made sure that you were smartly dressed. Poor, maybe, but proud nonetheless. This era was a difficult one for the ordinary working classes, simply because so many of them joined the non working classes. A worldwide recession meant that there was little to boost the economy as production and manufacturing fell. Workers were laid off and families struggled to make ends meet in the period that became known as 'the Depression'. Such difficult times bred unrest. There were anti-establishment riots on the streets and protest marches galore, including the famous Jarrow March to London in 1936. Some people turned to the likes of Oswald Mosley's British Union of Fascists for salvation, while others went the opposite way and joined the Communist Party.

Below: In 1936, the Queen's Hotel was in the early stages of construction with funding from London Midland and Scottish Railways. It opened the following March with a ceremony conducted by Henry Lascelles, the 6th Earl of Harewood and husband of Mary, the Princess Royal and daughter of King George V. This hotel replaced the one built in 1863 for the Midland Railway Company. It was extended twice, in 1867 and 1898, but required a complete overhaul to bring it up to date for the demands of the 20th century. It was felt to be more cost effective to start all over again. Leeds Wellington Station was built in 1846 by the Bradford and Leeds Railway Company. Leeds New Station opened in 1869 and was jointly owned by North East Railway and London North West Railway. The two stations were combined in 1938 as Leeds City Station and completely rebuilt in 1967. The statue of the Black Prince in the centre of the square is something of an anomaly. There is no evidence that he ever had any real connection with, or lands, in the area. In 1893 Leeds gained city status and, the following year, the Lord Mayor decided to erect the statue to mark the occasion. Apparently, he felt that the son of King Edward III symbolised all sorts of civic virtues, among them democracy, good government and chivalry. It was not until 1903 that the statue was unveiled.

Above: A horse and cart stood outside Miller and Page's Furniture Galleries on Albion Street on this day in 1935. Despite the advent of the internal combustion engine, original examples of horsepower were still common sights on our roads. Even after the war, we would often see brewery drays and farmers' carts on their way to market. Rag and bone men could be found bowling along the back streets, swapping a housewife's cast offs for a donkeystone to whiten the front step. In the 1930s, the lot of the working classes was still one of a struggle against poverty. Lloyd George had promised 'a land fit for heroes' after World War I, but it never materialised. For many, things did not get better and unemployment rose to record levels during the 1930s. The lucky ones who had regular jobs enjoyed better circumstances and the gap between the haves and have nots widened. Skilled workers could earn a weekly wage of between £3 5s and £3 15s and unskilled ones between £2 10s and £2 15s. Although these seem pittances today, in real terms they were more than enough to live on. They represented a rise of over a third in purchasing power when compared with pay packets in the early 1920s. It was estimated that a couple with four children could live on £2 per week, so there was plenty left over for extras, provided that you had a job.

Above: It was a bright summer's afternoon in 1947 when the Griffin Hotel on the corner of Boar Lane and Mill Hill was photographed. It wasn't the only time the sun shone that summer. Day after day brought glorious weather as Britain basked in a heatwave. The term 'global warming' had not been invented; this was just a welcome blip in the country's meteorological format. Trains and coaches were packed as trippers set off to Scarborough, Filey and Bridlington to enjoy themselves in the Mediterranean-like weather. Not that many knew what the climate on the Med felt like, since foreign travel was for the toffee-nosed and well-heeled. It would be another decade or more before the package holiday to foreign parts became part of ordinary people's culture. At least the sunshine made us forget rationing, cutbacks and privations for a while. It was in complete contrast to the problems the country faced earlier that winter. Heavy snowstorms and sub-zero temperatures, combined with a serious fuel shortage, brought the country to its economic knees. Come the summer, all that was forgotten on the cricket field as the Brylcreem Boy, Denis Compton, ran amok, scoring 3,816 runs for Middlesex. The Griffin Hotel was the venue where some members of Hunslet soccer club met in 1904 to found Leeds City Association Football Club. They also sanctioned the purchase of Holbeck Rugby Club's Elland Road ground to function as their headquarters. Leeds City played in the Football League until 1919.

Below: Lewis's store was fronting an appeal fund for Leeds General Infirmary in this 1934 photograph of The Headrow. The RAC sign on the lamppost in the distance pointed towards Headingley where the fourth Test was being played. This tells us that the photograph dates from July in that year. Crowds would have been enormous as the Australians provided the opposition. Ashes' games have always been the best supported and most keenly contested of cricket matches. Unlike today, the game was played over four days, though they could have got in as many overs as we see now, since the rate of play was far quicker back then. The home side was captained by RES Wyatt and contained several players who were or would become among the best in the world.

Wally Hammond was an outstanding batsman, Les Ames a wicket keeper who became the first in his position to score a test century, Harrogate's Maurice Leyland was an accomplished strokemaker and Bill Bowes a fine fast bowler from Elland. The Australians had the peerless Don Bradman amongst their number. His superb knock of 304 dominated proceedings and England was lucky to escape with a draw. Across from Lewis's, the appearance of George Robey on stage would have attracted a large audience. The 'Prime Minister of Mirth' possessed superb comic timing that was also suited to classic straight acting. He appeared in light operetta during the 1930s, having forsaken revue. He was knighted in 1954, a few months before his death.

Below: By late 1944, the tide was turning in favour of the Allies as a second front was established in France. German troops left the Channel Islands and our forces broke through the Siegfried line on the mainland. In the Far East, General MacArthur returned to the Philippines as he had promised. There was still much to be done and some setbacks along the way, as when the assault on Arnhem proved to be an expensive failure, but a mood of optimism swept Britain for the first time in five years. Looking along The Headrow from the junction with Briggate and towards Eastgate, the Odeon was showing one of the smash box office hits of the year. There had been a number of popular films with a wartime theme that had a certain propaganda element, but this one was completely different. Perhaps it represented our need for something truly uplifting amongst the immorality of war and all the misery it brought. 'The Song of Bernadette' told the story of the peasant girl, Bernadette Soubirous (1844-79), who had several visions of the Virgin Mary in 1858 in her home village of Lourdes. These appearances inspired the pilgrimages in search of miraculous cures that continue today. The movie won several Oscars, including one for its star, Jennifer Jones, who portrayed Bernadette with a sensitivity that touched the heart of even the most cynical cinemagoer.

Above: The Leeds and Holbeck Building Society and Liverpool Victoria Insurance Offices stood on either side of the Albion Street junction with The Headrow. The former was formally established in 1875, but its origins began 30 years earlier. In January 1845 a group of people formed the Leeds Union Operative Land and Building Society. Members regularly contributed towards shares. When there were sufficient funds, a ballot was held and a beneficiary was granted the necessary advance to buy a property. This procedure was repeated until all members were satisfied. In total, four Holbeck Societies were established and terminated. In 1875 Leeds and Holbeck (Permanent) Building Society was founded by share holders of the original societies. By the end of the first year, 450 accounts had been opened and a distribution of £16,000 in mortgage funds was made. It has since grown into one of the top 10 such societies in the country. In March 2005, at the Society's Annual General Meeting, the name was changed to the Leeds Building Society. Liverpool Victoria is similar in age, having been founded in 1843, and has grown into Britain's largest friendly society. In 1951, sitting close to these large financial institution, we could have visited Eastwood's broken pipe mender's shop. Any pipe smoker will tell you of his annoyance in snapping the stem when a favourite briar dropped to the floor or was caught in his jacket when closing the car door. Rescue was at hand here.

Above: The Queen's Hotel stands behind the tram shelter as we look east along City Square in the direction of Boar Lane. It was 1946 and some of the kerbs and lampposts still retained the white bands and markings painted on them as a guide during the blackout. The elegant hotel, with its 217 bedrooms on 8 floors, opened in 1937 as a replacement to the former hotel that was built in 1863 for the Midland Railway Company. Some of the bedrooms looked across the square at the torch bearing statues of 'Morn' and 'Even'. The Queen's Palm Court was renowned for its superior quality afternoon teas, as well as being the place to see and be seen in. Rationing was still in force in 1946 and genteel luncheons had to be more modest affairs than those before the war. No meal could cost more than five shillings (25p in today's money) and chefs had to be quite imaginative with the limited resources at their disposal. It was some years before we really got back to normal, though with the coming of peace at least such revolting meals as Woolton pie were well behind us. That particular main course recipe came from the Ministry of Food's boss, Lord Woolton, and was comprised of carrots, turnips, parsnips and potatoes in an oatmeal stock and was crowned by a pastry or potato crust and served with watery brown gravy. There is no record that the mighty Marquis ever ate it himself.

The cables crisscrossing Boar Lane, as seen from its junction with Briggate in 1943, remind us that the tram was still an important part of public transport. Trams of one form or another ran in Leeds from September 1871 and were to make an enormous contribution to the public transport system of the city for the next 88 years. On 29 October 1891, Leeds became the first city in the United Kingdom to operate electric trams on the overhead wire system. These became a familiar part of city life until they finally passed into history on a cold, foggy night in November 1959. The blue and cream livery, in latter years it became red and cream, was an attractive sight on the city streets. Leeds has always been at the vanguard of innovation. In 1911 it was the first place to employ trolleybuses as part of its transport fleet. The original idea was a 'trackless tram' that would save the cost of laying lines but would have the advantages of electric traction. After various methods of current collection, the twin trolleyboom and twin overhead wire system became the norm. However, it was in Wolverhampton that the first trolleybuses to actually look like a bus, rather than a tram, appeared. This wartime picture shows few private vehicles on the street as petrol was rationed and only used for essential journeys.

Above: In the early 1930s 'talkies' were still a modern phenomenon, so it was no surprise to see a billboard heavily promoting the fact the 'Rainbow Man' was a movie with sound. It had little else to recommend it and its memory has faded into complete obscurity, but at the time its novelty value would have been of use in attracting an audience. There is a real mix of modern 1930s and days gone by in this photograph of City Square. On one side of the road a man pushes a small dustcart as he carefully goes about his business, sweeping the gutters. Several horses and carts vie for space with up to the minute saloon cars and lorries, while tramcars, full of passengers, make their way along the square towards the Royal Exchange Building. A policeman on point duty beckons a car across the tramlines on its way out of the city. The foreground belongs to the memorial to those who fell in the Great War, as World War I was then known. It cost £5,000, a small price to pay to remember the thousands who made the ultimate sacrifice. The figure of Winged Victory hovered above Peace, in the form of a female figure bearing an olive branch, and War, represented by St George slaying the Dragon. As traffic congestion increased, the memorial was moved to the Garden of Remembrance.

Below: The cars in the photograph are reminiscent of those in 'The Untouchables', the popular television programme from the 1960s that described police work against the gangsters in Chicago during the prohibition years. The vehicles were all running boards and externally mounted spare wheels, just like the ones in this view of The Headrow, seen from Albion Street, as it appeared in 1934. Lewis's department store on the left was only 18 months old, but had already built up a faithful clientele that would stay true for half a century until the decline set in. This scene is from a world that is out of the experience of all except the most mature of readers. Some things that we take for granted today were in their infancy. The second soccer World Cup took place in Italy, where the host country was victorious. England would not be represented in this tournament until 1950. At home, the Road Traffic Bill introduced the driving test and plans were made to bring in pedestrian crossings and install Percy Shaw's invention, cats' eyes, in road surfaces. The GPO decided to introduce postal districts and the future author Alan Bennett was born in Armley. The gangster scene across the Atlantic kept the sensationalist press busy. Bonnie and Clyde were killed in a police ambush and Public Enemy Number One, John Dillinger, was gunned down outside a cinema.

It was 8.23 in the morning and rush hour was not fully over on Briggate as the photographer aimed his lens over the subterranean public toilets. Shoppers had not arrived in any number as yet, though many of the office workers and shop assistants were already in place. In 1938, Burton's, the 'tailor of taste', and the Fifty Shilling Tailor stood side by side in competition for the role of principal menswear store. The Montague Burton (1885-1952) chain of stores advanced rapidly from humble beginnings at the start of the last century. He acquired a huge factory in Leeds in 1925, employing 10,000 workers and was said to open a new shop every month in the 20s and 30s. By World War II he was clothing a quarter of the male population. He was knighted in 1931. Locally born Henry Price (1877-1963) was the founder of the Fifty Shilling Tailor men's outfitter. He acknowledged that, despite money being tight in the interwar years, men still wanted to dress as elegantly as they could afford and he spotted a niche in the market. Price established his chain, selling cheap, but acceptable, clothing. Soon he had stores across the country that remained popular throughout the 1950s until greater prosperity and a desire for more fashionable clothing altered purchasing patterns. Price was knighted in 1937 and, after his passing, left a legacy of fond memories of the days when his suits cost just £2.50, in today's terminology.

Above: Mill Hill Chapel was in need of restoration and the scaffolding in front of the building suggests that work had begun. It was consecrated in 1848, but needed urgent repairs by May 1955 and an appeal for £40,000 was launched. There had been a Unitarian chapel on Mill Hill since 1674 and that long connection with the site continues today. This branch of Christianity began in 1662 when 2,000 clergymen were ejected from the Church of England because they would not be bound by the Book of Common Prayer. The congregations were known as Presbyterian until the 19th century when they adopted the Unitarian name. One of the most eminent of Mill Hill ministers was the Rev Joseph Priestley, who was born at Birstall in March 1733 into a weaving family.

His work as a scientist of renown led to his memory being commemorated by the statue close by on City Square, from where he looks across to the chapel. Other notable buildings seen here include Barclays Bank, the Post Office and the Norwich Union offices. City Square was laid out in 1903 and, although there have several facelifts since then, it still provides the visitor with a favourable impression when entering the square for the first time.

Left: The mock Tudor frontage of the shops in New Briggate presented an attractive sight in the early 1960s. However, the disposition of some of the proprietors was not as sunny as the day on which this scene was captured. A notice in the window at Judson's Electronics advertised a 'Demolition Sale'. Briggate is one of the city's most prestigious streets. Meaning 'road to the bridge', it was at the heart of the town laid out following the charter of 1207. An early 19th century map shows a series of narrow yards opening off both sides of the street along the whole of its length. This reflects the layout of the old burgage plots from medieval times. Briggate had been the centre of trade in Leeds, with merchants living in the houses lining the street and the building of the first Moot Hall, the centre of judicial and council administration.

The market and administrative offices moved out of Briggate in Victorian times as it became a shopping centre for aspiring middle classes. However, it lost its influence as The Headrow grew in importance and by the 1930s was a sad shadow of its former self. Regeneration towards the end of the last century has helped it reclaim much of its former glory.

Above: We are in the heart of the swinging sixties in this photograph, looking across City Square. The Queen's Hotel is on the left and the towering presence of the Post Office dominates the skyline to the right. In 1964, the country was in a state of change. The complacent Tory party had been sent to the opposition benches and replaced by Harold Wilson's Labour government. A new breed of voters had had enough of the establishment politics that it considered more suitable to the elderly and upper classes. Instead, it turned to the more down to earth, pragmatic approach that Wilson appeared to present. The hole in the foreground marks the grave of the Royal Exchange that had stood on this side of City Square for over 90 years. Careful observation will reveal a white sleeved figure standing in a box as cars pass by him. This bobby was on point duty, trying to keep things moving around the square. Like some marvellous mime artist, he beckoned and waved as he instructed traffic to move or wait for his next signal. We literally did have police on the streets in those days. The Black Prince, on his plinth in the centre, had looked out across this scene since 1903. The statue was the brainchild of Lord Mayor, Thomas Harding, who also provided the funds for its casting in Belgium.

AT LEISURE

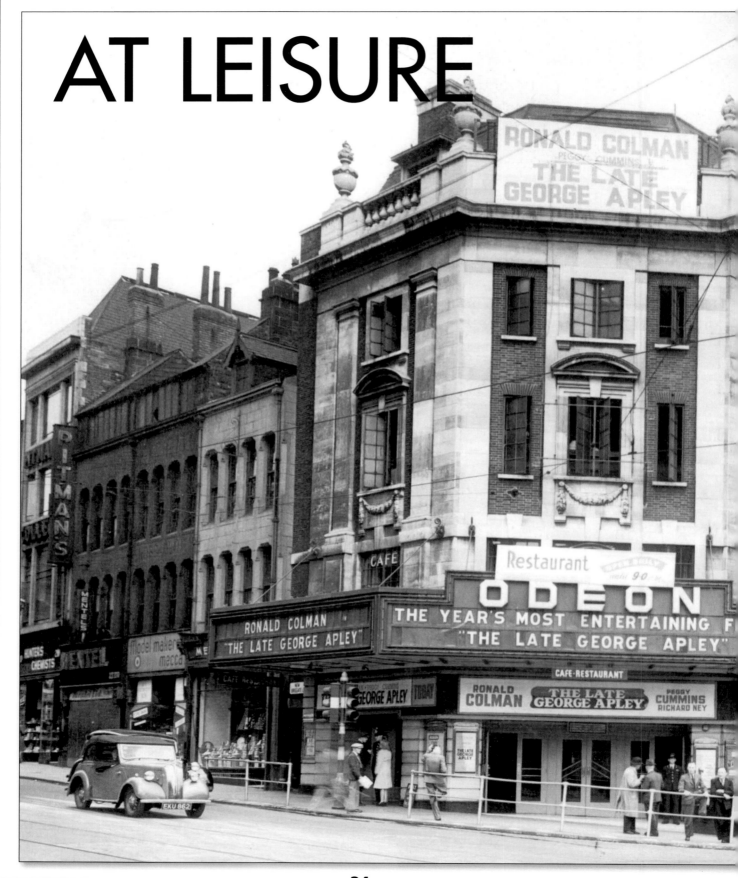

The Odeon Cinema, on this corner of The Headrow and New Briggate, proudly advertised its latest Ronald Colman film that was showing on 25 June 1947. Large audiences flocked to 'the flicks' 60 years ago during this period of the movie industry's heyday. Now we can enjoy Hollywood epics on our televisions, watch a DVD, view them through a computer and the technology is there to tune in via a mobile phone. But, when the Odeon packed them in, this was the place to go to see the latest sagas coming out of Tinseltown or our own Ealing, Shepperton and Pinewood studios. The film showing here, 'The Late George Apley', was a fairly ordinary offering, a comedy-drama about the family life of a Boston blueblood. However, its box office success was guaranteed because Ronald Colman played the lead. Born in Surrey in 1891, He fought at Ypres in World War I and was invalided out after being badly injured by shrapnel. By chance, after recovering from his wounds, he turned to the theatre. He progressed quickly through the acting ranks and became a top silent movie star. He was blessed with a melodious speaking voice and made the transition to 'talkies' with great success. He received an Academy Award for his splendid portrayal of a tormented actor in the 1947 film 'A Double Life', He died in 1958.

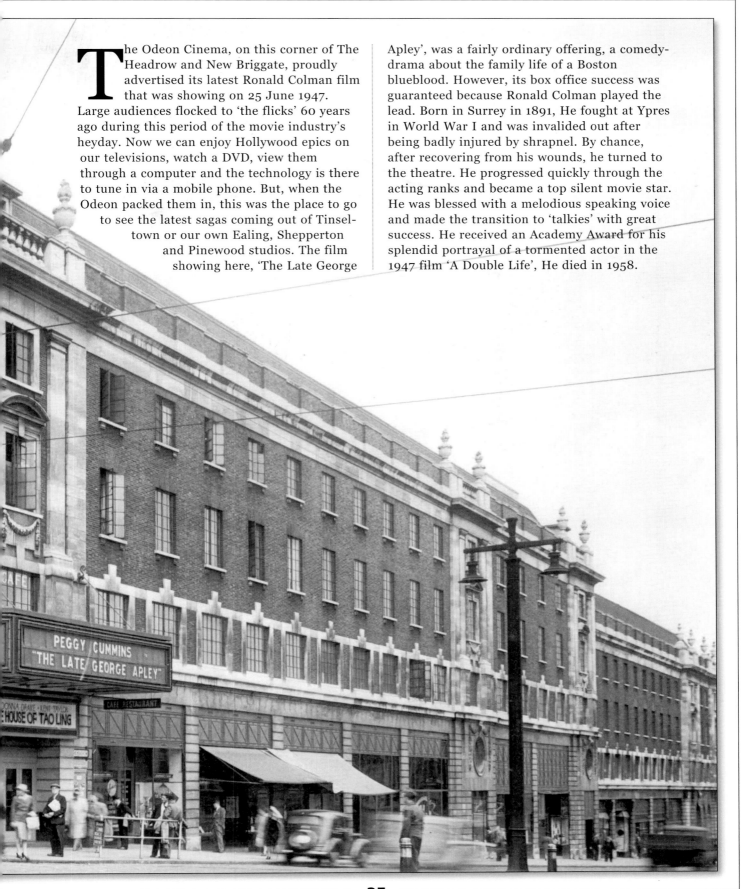

Below: These youngsters in the pools at Roundhay Park belong to the baby boomer years. Seen on 2nd June 1955, exactly two years after the Coronation, they are members of the large upsurge in population that saw the birthrate rise dramatically in the immediate postwar years. Many parents were reluctant to add to their families or start one at all during the war as who would wish to bring a child into the world during such uncertain times? Quite a large number had no opportunity to do so as the men were stationed overseas. But, when peace was declared and the boys came marching home, nature took its course. The stork's wings beat a steady route to the maternity hospitals throughout 1946 and 1947. There are so many baby boomers around now that there do not seem to be sufficient pension funds to cushion their advancing years. All that was beyond the children frolicking in the sun back then. Roundhay Park covers over 700 acres of parkland, lakes, woodland and gardens. During the 13th century it was hunting land for the De Lacy family. The estate was purchased by Thomas Nicholson in 1803 and, as the family had no heir, given to the people of Leeds in 1871. Roundhay also plays host to large open air events, one of which in 2006 closed schools and created huge traffic jams when Robbie Williams gave a two day concert.

Above: The rest garden on Merrion Street was an oasis of calm in the busy city centre. Here people could relax in the sunshine and let the cares of the world go by. It could have been part of a little market town somewhere in the Cotswolds rather than one of the country's largest centres of population. How tranquil the scene appears. There was no hustle and bustle for these people, or if there was then they were taking the 1940s' equivalent of time out. On 22 September 1943 there was much in the world that could have occupied their thoughts and perhaps they needed a few minutes' respite from the harsh reality of what was happening across Europe. It was whispered that some concentration camp inmates in Poland had been used as guinea pigs in extreme medical experiments. Surely not, they thought. It seemed hard to imagine that any human being could be so cruel to another. How naïve they were. In Italy, the Allies pushed up the heel of Italy and the Red Army started to hit back at the German invaders, recapturing several strategically important Russian towns. The tide was turning. On the home front, a new method of collecting income tax was announced. Instead of informing the Inland Revenue of your earnings, these would now be taxed at source under the PAYE scheme.

Below: Now these are proper children, just like most of us were once over. Not a sign of designer gear, ear pieces connected to a music centre or a mobile phone bulging in a side pocket. The little lad towards the rear of the group has a sticking plaster on his knee and his socks are heading in a downward spiral. You were a tad short of being a true boy if your knees lacked scabs. His short back and sides and cheeky grin firmly establish him in his role as a typical representative of 1950s boyhood, all slugs and snails and puppy dog tails. All the lads are in short trousers. They did not aspire to 'longs' until well into double figures. Some lanky 12 year olds looked a little incongruous in their shorts, but rules were rules. If the school banned full length trousers until you were in the fourth form, then that was that. It was also cheaper on mum's housekeeping, since cut knees grew new flesh, but torn trousers needed mending or replacing. The girls were just as traditional in their attire. No jeans or trousers for them. White ankle socks, patent leather strapover or lace-up shoes and knee length dresses were required. Adornment was limited to a bow, Alice band or plaited pigtails. The blonde in the middle was probably not too happy with the look of her National Health glasses, but at least they were not the pink ones that short sighted kids hated. The photograph was taken at Quarry Hill around the time of the 1953 Coronation, hence the commemorative mugs.

Top right: Journalists are well known for their enjoyment of the odd tipple. On 2 May 1962, this group of newspapermen who liked to frequent the Ostler's Arms looked at the headline from the Evening News. Shock, horror! The price of petrol was going up, perhaps by as much as 4d a gallon. That is less than 0.4p per litre at today's pumps. But, 45 years ago it cost just under five shillings (25p) per gallon, so the increase would have been the approxinmate equivalent of a price hike of 7p per litre on current levels. Selwyn Lloyd, the Chancellor of the Exchequer, was not a popular man with the motoring public. It is hard to think of any since who have been. The movement in the cost of motoring has continued upwards, with the biggest percentage jumps occurring in 1975 and 1980-81. The pipe smoker in the photograph chewed reflectively upon his briar as he considered the effect that the increase would have on his life. Did he ever contemplate that the day would come when he could not do such a thing in a public house? Branded unclean and tarred with the brush of criminality, heaven help the man who lights up a bowl full of St Bruno in this day and age. Cynics predict that in a few years' time pubs will be banned from selling beer as a means of combatting alcoholism and lager louts.

Right: You got good value for money at the cinema. There were usually two films showing, a newsreel, a short travelogue or information film and Tom and Jerry as well. On 14 March

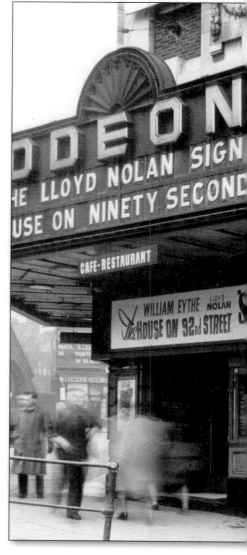

1946 you could see 'The House on Ninety Second Street', a film that would win an Oscar for Charles G Booth's original story line. It was a tale of the FBI foiling a Nazi wartime plot to steal atomic secrets. Leo G Carroll was one of the supporting cast of actors and is best remembered for playing the part of the section head, Mr Waverly, in TV's 'Man from UNCLE'. The B movie, 'Sun Valley Serenade', starred Sonja Henie, the former ice skater who won three gold medals at the 1928 Olympics. The Odeon was one of the biggest cinemas in the north. It was built as the Paramount by the chain of that name in 1932 with 2,590 seats. There were 1,580 stalls and 1,010 places in the circle. A Wurlitzer organ was installed at a cost of £20,000. The Paramount circuit was bought by Oscar Deutsch and its name changed to Odeon on 15 April 1940. A business friend of his spotted the name 'Odeon' in Tunis and recommended it, particularly as it started with Deutsch's initials. He died the following year and the company was later sold to J Arthur Rank.

WARTIME

At first sight this would appear to be the aftermath of an air raid. That is what you are meant to imagine as this actually was a mock-up of such an incident staged in Kirkstall on 10 July 1941. At the start of the war, civil defence groups practised what they would do in the event of an aerial attack. The general public was well aware, from newsreel footage, of the devastation that could be wreaked by the Luftwaffe. Visions from the Spanish Civil War, especially the Condor Division's razing of the pretty Basque town of Guernica in 1937, were clear in everyone's mind. Although Leeds escaped major damage, there being just nine attacks

of which just six were serious, complacency could not be permitted. So, the civil defence exercises continued. In total, 77 people were killed by bombing, 71 seriously injured and 249 slightly wounded by enemy action. An estimated 3,500 incendiaries and 14 high explosive bombs fell on the city during the first raid in the early hours of 1 September 1940. The worst attack took place on 14 March 1941. Casualty figures were often obscured in wartime to deny the Germans propaganda material, but postwar records suggest that 65 people were killed that night and 260 injured, 56 of them seriously. Some 4,600 houses were damaged to a degree, as were the Town Hall and City Museum.

Below: There are no glass bowls on the streetlamps along Centenary Street, sandbags are stacked against the walls and white markings have been painted on bollards, traffic lights and kerbstones. This is 1940 on The Headrow and the war is a year old. The bobby on point duty had an easy job as petrol rationing meant that there was little traffic about. The Art Gallery and Library building dominates the panorama. Leeds Library on Commercial Street was completed in 1808, but in 1884 various municipal functions, including the Central Library that stood on Infirmary Street, were combined in a new building. As Leeds had grown apace in Victorian times, the 1858 Town Hall was unable to accommodate all the various departments. A competition to design a new Town Hall was won by George Corson (1829-1910). The building has an Italian styling, with the front part that faces Calverley Street being particularly ornate. The north and south sides are plainer in design, as is the entrance to the Library on the south side. The Art Gallery was designed by WH Thorp and cost £10,000 to build. Colonel TW Harding was the driving force behind the movement to provide the town with an art collection and the money was eventually raised by public subscription. It opened in October 1888.

Above: Winston Churchill made a number of morale boosting visits to the provinces during World War II. Here, he had just left the Civic Hall, accompanied by his wife, in May 1942. They had married in September 1908. Clementine Hozier was a dazzling, but largely penniless, beauty whom he met at a dinner party that March. Her background was shrouded in a mixture of mystery and scandal. Officially, her parents were Sir Henry Montague Hozier and Lady Blanche (née Ogilvy). However, he was unable to have children and Clementine was variously thought to have been fathered by a certain Captain Middleton or her own brother in law, Algernon Mitford. Winston and Clementine had five children and their only son, Randolph, also entered politics. Winston Churchill (1874-1965) had a chequered and varied career, but eventually came to be regarded as one of the most influential Britons that have ever lived. At various times he was an author, soldier, journalist, legislator and painter. A descendant of the Dukes of Marlborough, like so many of his class, Churchill was packed off to boarding school as a youngster and spent an unhappy, lonely time as a youth. After graduating from Sandhurst, he worked as both a soldier and a reporter, but his main love was politics. In 1900, he became Oldham's MP and the love affair with power really began.

Above: It was party time for these residents of inner city Leeds. After six years of turmoil and anxiety, it was time to let their hair down. When victory in Europe was secured in May 1945, with Japan capitulating three months later, the Union flags and the bunting came out everywhere. A 'welcome home' message can be seen hanging over the heads of these locals, so one of their own must have been on his way back from some foreign field. It was a time to rejoice, because loved ones had been away for ages. Some might even have been parted for five years, with a husband, son or father incarcerated in a prisoner of war camp. All the joy was tempered with the knowledge that for some there would be no homecoming. They lay forever in a strange land, with only a headstone in a mass grave to mark their passing. They had paid the ultimate price so that, in other families, Jimmy could have his own little room again as the bluebirds flew overhead. The 'V for Victory' sign was the message with which Prime Minister Winston Churchill greeted the public as he sent out the optimistic and morale boosting greeting everywhere he went. Despite echoing the great man's sentiments, voters on this street and in the rest of the country voted Churchill out of office a fortnight before the war in the Far East ended.

Below: This street party in Manor Grove was held to celebrate the end of the second world war, though these festivities were not held until September, a month after the atom bombs were dropped on Hiroshima and Nagasaki. That action, though horrific in its carnage, ensured that hostilities did not drag on for months and saved the lives of many Allied troops both in the field and in captivity. Nearly everyone in the picture was making the 'V for Victory' sign, though by then its most famous user was consigned to the opposition benches. Clement Attlee replaced Churchill at 10 Downing Street in July 1945 and we did not see the great man at the helm of power again until 1951. Mums did their best with their meagre rations to provide a spread for the children. It was a case of standing room only as all the available chairs were taken. The tables were covered with neatly starched cloths and the decorations on top provided a jolly touch. We were free from the threat that the yoke of tyranny was to be placed around our necks, so we celebrated even harder than we had for the King's coronation in 1937. One sobering message amongst the festivities came from the sight of the young man in a wheelchair, centre right. Was he one of the casualties of war? We know of the countless thousands who died during those years, but there were also many, many others whose lives were blighted by having to adjust as amputees, the sightless and the mentally scarred.

Large water tanks were placed along The Headrow during the second world war as a backup for the fire service to use in case mains supply was disrupted during a bombing raid. By October 1944, the worst of the assault on Britain from the air was over, though London and the south coast still had to endure the flying bombs and rockets coming over from Peenemunde. The fire service was but one branch of the civil defence that helped us get through those dark days of the early 1940s. Braving the fires raging round them and the falling masonry that could have crushed them at any moment, firefighters were supported by police, ambulance crews and volunteers from the Women's Voluntary Service, Red Cross, St John Ambulance, Home Guard and many other groups. These services, some career based and others born of civic duty, worked hand in hand to the common end. They were 'doing their bit' for the war effort, sometimes at great cost to their own personal safety. Leeds was more fortunate than most cities in terms of the volume of air raids it had to endure. Lacking the heavy industry and port status of such as London, Liverpool, Birmingham, Coventry, Exeter, Glasgow, Manchester, Southampton and Portsmouth, Leeds was only subjected to nine aerial assaults during World War II. They were nine too many, but only a fraction of those endured elsewhere.

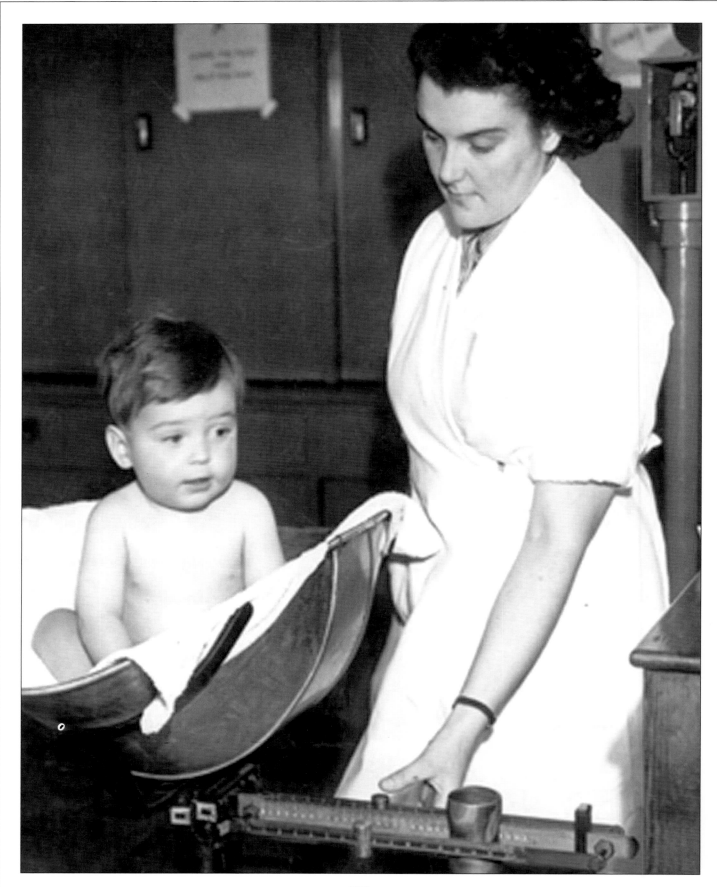

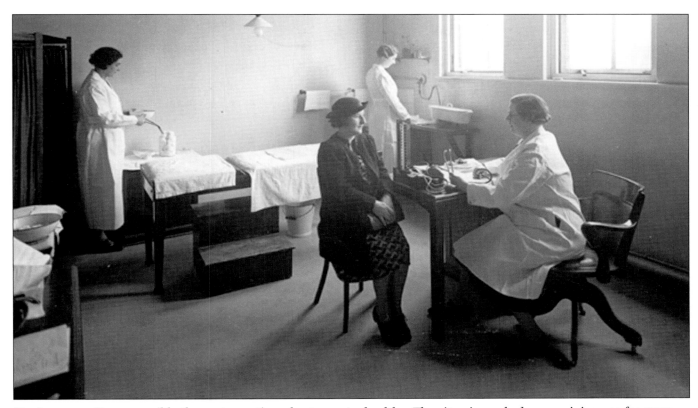

Both pages: It was possibly the acute wartime shortages of food and supplies which made doctors, health workers and mothers alike very aware of the health of the new generation, and children were carefully weighed, measured and immunised against the illnesses that had at one time meant disfigurement or even death *(facing page)*. A vaccine for polio, the scourge of former years which left behind its terrible mark of wasted and useless limbs, only came later, however. American scientist Jonas Edward Salk developed a vaccine in 1955, and an oral vaccine was produced in 1960. The vaccines brought the dreaded disease under control and today polio is rarely seen. On a day to day basis, vitamins were vital to the health of children, and long before the advent of the cod liver oil capsule, the recommended spoonful of cod liver oil was administered to the youngest children every day in schools and nurseries around the country during the 1940s. Children might have screwed up their noses at the fishy taste, but the nourishing cod liver oil went a long way towards keeping them healthy. The vitamin-packed orange juice was far more palatable, and artful mothers would often use the orange juice as a bribe: no cod liver oil, no orange juice. Following hard on the heels of the oil, the juice took away the distinctive taste that was disliked by so many children. Ante-natal clinics did all they could to check on the diet, blood pressure and vitamin intake of mothers to be; our carefully posed photograph *(top)*, taken in an ante-natal clinic in the 1930s, records at least the cleanliness and tidiness that was to their great credit. And when the tiny new citizen finally arrived, there were health visitors to pay friendly calls on families in their homes to check on the health and happiness of mothers and babies *(left)*. National Dried Milk for babies was also made available to mothers, and before today's push towards natural feeding NDM was for decades very much in vogue. We need to remember that at the time of these photographs the National Health service did not exist, and in fact the NHS only came into operation after World War II in July 1948.

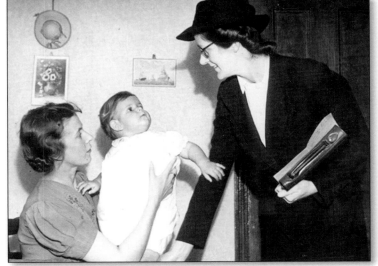

Armstrong Priestley - Life savers

In 1975 a Yeadon-based plumber and builder, Ron Priestley, had to supply a fire sprinkler protection system to a small shop in Huddersfield. Never one to place himself at the mercy of a specialist Ron contacted Peter Armstrong, a former maths and science teacher, who had recently been made redundant by a major sprinkler installer. On completion of their first job together Ron and Peter decided to look for more work of the same kind: almost by accident Armstrong Priestley was founded.

The company's first client was Sherbourne Pouffes in Bradford and now 30 years later Sherbourne Upholstery are still loyal clients.

Today, based at prestigious premises, 'Seventy Seven' in Holbeck Lane, Leeds, where the company moved in 2006, Armstrong Priestley is one of the UK's leading Fire Protection Contractors. As specialists in the design, installation, servicing and maintenance of automatic fire sprinklers, the company has tailor-made automatic sprinkler systems for both public and private sector clients for over 30 years.

Though the company now has more than 60 permanent employees, and another dozen sub-contract workers, the business was far more modest at its inception with just Peter Armstrong carrying out the installation work with his friend

Brian Bartram helping out with designs. But what exactly are fire sprinklers, and who invented them?

The earliest sprinkler patents date from the 18th Century. The modern 'automatic' system has its origins in the invention (in the 1870s) of a sprinkler head, which would open in response to heat. Although it was unreliable and suffered from problems with debris clogging the parts, Henry S. Parmalee's invention provided the first practical 'automatic sprinkler'.

Frederick Grinnell in 1878 patented the design, which has

Above: *Co founders, Peter Armstrong and Ron Priestley.*
Below: *Company Secretary Hilary Lee, circa 1980.*
Above right: *John Moore who has been with the company for 27 years pictured in the mid 1980s.*
Right: *Old fire sprinklers.*

dramatically. Grinnell produced its first 'modern' type in 1922 and other manufacturers followed suit.

It was not until 1957 that attention turned to producing a sprinkler which would respond more rapidly to a fire. Sprinklers have enjoyed mixed fortunes since their invention, being liked by insurance companies and the fire fighting community but not by some owners and developers. American statistics show that fire related losses are reduced by up to some 43 percent when sprinklers are installed – inclusive of any 'water damage', and the risks of accidental discharge and leakage can be reduced significantly by proper installation and maintenance.

About 99 percent of all fire reported in sprinklered premises in the United Kingdom in which the system actuated, were controlled or extinguished by the system. Of these, 60 percent were controlled by four heads or less with a few cases being reported where more than 24 heads operated.

become the pattern for subsequent developments. His design originally produced a sprinkler with a solder strut as its heat sensitive actuator and the only major modification to the basic pendent sprinkler head for almost 50 years, was the introduction of the quartzoid bulb. Most modifications since then have focused on the deflector plate producing a variety of spray patterns and, since the 1920's, on the metal bulk of the heads themselves.

Early heads were very bulky with the solder strut or glass bulb shrouded by the metal. It was not appreciated until the 1920's that this actually delayed the response

But to return to Armstrong Priestley Ltd.

When the business began in 1976 it operated from just one room in a shop in Yeadon. By 1978 however, more space was needed and Armstrong Priestley moved to the former railway station in Headingley. By then Ron Priestley had left the company in order to concentrate on property development.

Hilary Lee joined the business in 1979. Her first job was to acquire a desk, a chair and a typewriter, not to mention carpets and heating. In due course, Hilary became both Company Secretary and Peter Armstrong's partner.

Also joining the business at Headingley Station were John Moore as a trainee draftsman and Laurie Morse who dealt with sales and estimating. The then young John Moore was interested in computers and introduced them to the company. John would become the company's IT Manager as well as a partner with Peter Armstrong in Canute, a computer software company. Laurie Morse would become Sales Director and remain with the company until 2005 when he retired to pursue his interest in mountaineering. Today the Sales and Marketing is under the control of Terry Bennett.

The year 1986 saw a move to much larger office/workshop premises – Flaxton House in Beeston. It was at this point that a young typist, Anne Marie Dempsey, joined the company in a very junior role. Now Mrs Anne Marie Cable is the Financial Director and plays a major role in the continuing success of Armstrong Priestley aided and abetted by Karen Taylor as General Manager. Two ladies making an impression in what is essentially a man's world.

Armstrong Priestley would develop an unrivalled reputation amongst Yorkshire-based manufacturers, retail

Right: *Armstrong Priestley's are proud to say that Sherbourne Pouffes Ltd, their first customer in the 1970s, is still a loyal and valued customer today.*
Below: *Members of staff pictured outside the company's Headingley premises in the 1980s.*

developers and warehouse providers, as the industry's most dependable contractor.

In the 21st century Armstrong Priestley's reputation still rests upon an ability to control the reliability of both system design and installation - it still fabricates its systems in-house and still employs and trains its own industry-regulated workforce.

The company's ability to manage a project, from conceptual design, to acquiring planning and regulatory permission, including the manufacture of its own designs, ensures that projects are brought in on time and on budget.

Clients include Next Distribution, Education Leeds, Exel Logistics, United Biscuits, Crown Aerosols, McCain Foods, Merrion Centre, Leeds Shopping Plaza, Ostler Centre, Bradford and RAF Menwith Hill.

Currently the Company is extensively involved in protecting schools throughout Yorkshire and nationwide. To this end the Company has the support of the Fire Service and interestingly installations have been carried out in three fire stations.

From listed buildings, which include Cuthbert Broderick's famous Corn Exchange to No 1 City Square, the company provides unobtrusive yet life-saving systems which harmonise with both classic design and modernist architecture.

When a building comes forward for a change of use, it often provides challenges for the Fire Service. This was undoubtedly the case with a hostel in Leeds. The building had previously been an old people's home, which had been closed for six months. The property was to be reopened as a 34-bedroom hostel. It soon became evident that a substantial amount of fire protection work would be required to bring the building up to modern standards. It was with this in mind, that the Fire Service suggested a residential sprinkler installation as an alternative to passive fire protection. Not only was the installation of the sprinkler system less expensive but it also would have additional benefits.

It is likely that in the event of a fire only one sprinkler would operate, minimising the amount of water discharged on to the fire and so reducing the consequential loss and inconvenience. In fact a room protected with a sprinkler can often be reused in a matter of hours.

Residential sprinkler installations are relatively new in the UK although there are a growing number of fire authorities, which are actively supporting their use, together with interest from national government, particularly where houses of multiple occupation (HMOs) are involved. Many other countries throughout the world have recognised the benefits of residential sprinklers, particularly the United States where such installations are commonplace. A survey carried out by the Operational Life Safety organisation in the United States collected information on more than 600 fires in residential accommodation protected by sprinklers. Out of all these fires, there was not one reported fatality - compelling evidence that fire sprinkler systems can protect life as well as property.

Above: *Flaxton House, former premises of Armstrong Priestley.* **Inset:** *How the premises looked before renovation.*

Each contract for which the company tenders has to be dealt with in its own merits, and designed from first principles. There are no 'off the peg' solutions for sprinkler systems. Armstrong Priestley has its own team of designers with their own computer facilities for coping with the present trend towards fully hydraulically calculated installations.

It is a common fallacy, of course, that when a sprinkler system operates, water comes out of all the sprinkler heads. In fact, sprinkler installations are only designed for a maximum of 18 or 48 sprinkler heads to operate. This number is determined by the risk that is being protected. Statistics show that most fires are controlled by the operation of two or three sprinkler heads. The idea of a sprinkler installation is to control the fire until such time as the Fire Brigade can be in attendance.

The water is supplied by either the towns main or a storage tank holding sufficient water to supply the operating heads for an hour and a half.

Incredible though it may seem, often the installation of sprinklers is not even considered until the shop or the building is open for business and it is this type of situation the traditional large companies were unable to deal with.

The pace of life in the construction industry has increased considerably in the last few years, and Armstrong Priestley's ability to cope with this situation has been a major contributor to its expansion. The company is able to turn out quotations within a very short space of time from enquiry, and once the design is completed, can keep up with the builders and other trades on site. This is done by employing its own labour, contrary to the trend within the industry, which is to make use of sub-contract labour. The directors feel that sub-contact labour leads to all sorts of problems on site because of the difficulty of control and supervision. At the Holbeck premises, not only are there estimating and design facilities, but also a fabrication shop, so that the company is not dependant upon outside fabricators.

Each team of men at Armstrong Priestley have their own vehicle, fully equipped with all the necessary tools to do the job, and the fitters are experienced men who can cope with slight deviations to design without the necessity of constant reference back to the office.

In many ways the fitters are considered the Company's biggest asset, they are the ambassadors of the company, and the people with whom the client has most contact. Often clients ring and ask for a particular fitter by name, almost as though he were the only employee. The Company does not employ any sales people, the philosophy being that everybody within the company is a sales person and should present themselves and act accordingly.

Traditionally, the sprinkler industry has been looked upon as the lowest form in mechanical services, 'the pits of

Above right: *A 1995 staff photograh.*
Right: *The company's former Headingley premises.*

pipework'. The services 'show piece' in a building was a heating installation and complex boiler house.

In modern times heating is provided by small modular units dotted around the building. The predominant pipework, however, is the sprinkler installation, and it is the Company's aim to try and upgrade and status of the sprinkler industry to be at least on par with the heating trade. This can only do this by taking pride in the work undertaken and constantly trying to improve the standards of both design and installation.

To the majority of people the installation of sprinklers is an unwelcome interruption. It never enters people's minds that sprinklers could save their lives or their jobs. The only person to offer any welcome is the financial man who sees the tremendous saving in his insurance premiums.

The sprinkler installation, therefore, is an investment, a contribution towards profitability as well as safety, and it is important that the installation is maintained in an efficient working order. So often, expensive pump houses and installation control valves are completely neglected. Armstrong Priestley offer full servicing facilities and after sales service with a 24 hour call out facility.

The insurance companies play an important part in the sprinkler industry and since it is they who are giving the premium reductions, they vet the design and the installation of the system and carry out regular annual checks. The trends in insurance, therefore, do have some effect on the business activities of

Armstrong Priestley. When premiums are low there is less incentive for companies to allocate expenditure to Fire Protection, but when the market hardens, the enquiry rate increases.

The building trade has a similar effect on contractors like Armstrong Priestley. Obviously if no large buildings are being erected, then the need for fire protection decreases. These factors have to be borne in mind when the directors are planning for the following year.

With regard to the future the Company is not looking to take over the world, but to consolidate its position as the leading sprinkler installation company in the Yorkshire area and grow steadily as it has done in the past.

But sprinklers are not Armstrong Priestley only interest. The Company tries to take an active interest in the community and has in the past sponsored a young rally driver and a Leeds Rugby League player, currently sponsoring a youth football team in Kippax. The Company's main sponsorship however, is of The Grove and Rawdon Theatre Company and many Clients enjoy corporate evenings involving their productions.

Peter Armstrong is Chairman of BAFSA, the British Automatic Fire Sprinkler Association and Treasurer of the Sprinkler Engineers' Society. Peter is also a Director of the Fire Industry Confederation and has devoted a great deal of his time to promoting the industry in general.

Meanwhile Armstrong Priestley continues to set standards and has become the leading industry contractor in Yorkshire and the North East.

Top left: Fire Sprinkler Pump House. **Inset:** *Modern sprinklers.* **Below:** *Armstrong Priestley's prestigious Seventy Seven Holbeck Lane premises, 2006.*

Trams still rattled along Boar Lane in April 1951. The clanking car in the foreground had just passed the White Horse restaurant on the right. The last of these public transport vehicles ran in 1959 and with their demise an era came to an end. No more would we see the sight of the conductor at the end of one leg of a journey pull on the cord that swung the pantograph. This collector of electricity from the overhead cables was pivoted to face in the opposite direction. The driver then disconnected the brake and steering handles and remounted them at the other end of the car, ready to make the return journey. Looking over the top of the tram, the building with the Schweppes advert dominates the corner with Briggate. It was also an outlet for the prestigious Sheffield silversmith and cutlery firm of Walker and Hall. The company was established in 1840 by cutler George Walker and Henry Hall joined forces with him eight years later. They acquired the manufacturing silversmiths Henry Wilkinson and Company in 1892 and flourished as a leading name in the business during the first half of the 20th century. Walker and Hall combined with several others to form British Silverware in 1963. The Walker and Hall name was later revived as a retail firm.

SHOPPING SPREE

Above: Shoppers carefully hoarded their ration coupons as they saved up enough to be able to buy the essentials at Lewis's. This department store was established on The Headrow in September 1932 and soon built up a faithful clientele. However, when this photograph was taken in March 1949, clothing rationing had just been abolished. Women, in particular, responded with glee. Tired of the constraints forced upon them during the privations of the war years and their immediate successors, they turned their heads towards Paris. No longer would they have to put up with the 'make do and mend' culture. Women became expert at repairing, altering garments and making their own clothes. Pillowcases were made into baby clothes, father's old trousers became a skirt for his daughter and old parachute silk was much prized as material to make blouses and nightdresses. To save material, men's jackets had fake pockets and trousers had turn-ups. But now, fashion rather than necessity could take over. Christian Dior's New Look had already been introduced and now women could adopt it without the need for ration books. The hour-glass shape was reintroduced and ultra feminine figure-of-eight clothing was a delight to behold after years of drab utility wear. Hemlines fell to mid-calf length and soft shoulders and handspan waists became the rage. Lewis's traded success-fully until the 1980s when it went into a decline. The store closed in 1991 and was later home to Owen and Owen before Allders moved in.

Below: The 1950s were difficult years for the nation. It had gone through the immediate postwar changes that ushered in a Labour government who nationalised everything in sight, but failed to put an end to rationing or dispel people's fears about the growing menace of communism and its nuclear threat. These were indeed austere times. A lack of investment at home was natural since everything had been committed to the war effort. But now we had to pay the price. We were in hock to the Americans and it also took most of this decade to rebuild the homes and town centres flattened in bombing raids. Gradually, Britain began to turn the corner and production began to outstrip home demand and exports became important to the economy again. By the time Harold Macmillan was in power, we were able to support his assertion that we 'had never had it so good'. Unemployment figures fell steadily during the 1950s and we were able to squirrel away some savings into the Midland Bank at West Bar on Boar Lane. This handsome and ornately decorated building just oozed a feeling of opulence and wealth that inspired confidence. In the distance we can see one of Boot's stores. This was pulled down a few years after this scene was captured. Note that in the foreground we can see policemen on the street. Now there's a novelty!

Above: On Kirkgate in July 1956, shoppers vied with moving traffic and parked cars as they attempted to enjoy their day in the city centre. It was on Kirkgate that Michael Marks laid the foundations for the Marks and Spencer empire by opening his first market stall, the Penny Bazaar, in 1884. Kirkgate Market began as an open market at Vicar's Croft in the early 19th century. The covered one was opened in 1857 and was an impressive mixture of iron and glass, covering an area of 4.040 yards. At night this beautiful crystal market hall is well illuminated by 200 gas lights, arranged round handsome cast iron pillars. Here we are looking down towards Briggate, with Littlewood's store on the left. This was one of the chain that grew from the success of the football pools company founded by John Moores in 1923. A mail order business was started in 1932 and, using the profits to diversify, he opened his first department store in Blackpool in 1937. The Index group, its catalogue arm, opened in 1985, but the Littlewoods empire went into decline in the 1990s. It had struggled to keep pace with the increasingly competitive retail market and was bought out by the Barclay brothers in 2002. Three years later, many of the stores were sold off with large job losses ensuing.

Below: The notice on the side of I Stephenson's shop on the right hand corner tells us that here was a meat purveyor. This form of description was archaic even for the summer of 1956 when this view along Kirkgate was taken. The barber's shop above was also an old fashioned one. Here you could get either a short back and sides or a short back and sides. A dab of Brylcreem to make you look a bit like Denis Compton was about as trendy as it got. Teddy boy quifs and long sideburns had not taken over just yet, but they were on their way. Allied to the drainpipe trousers, luminous green socks and crepe-soled shoes, new fashions for young men were not too far away. The day of the teenager, a word seldom heard before, was waxing. This generation would start to rail against the norms of society and refuse to be mere mini clones of their parents. The baby boomers who followed a few years later would complete the process in the mid 1960s. The clash of tastes and styles would cause some family frictions. Fathers used to wearing conventional suits would not understand the Italian cut favoured by their sons and even less their taste in music. The pop charts in 1956 showed that, as Bob Dylan would later say, 'the times they are a-changing'. Crooners like Pat Boone and Ronnie Hilton topped the hit parade, but so did Frankie Lymon and the Teenagers. Elvis Presley took 'Heartbreak Hotel' and 'Blue Suede Shoes' into the top 10 and dads started to shout, 'Turn that row down!'

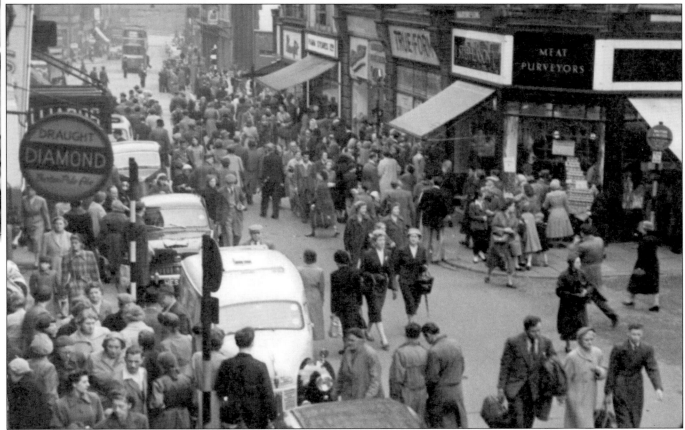

Right: The below knee hemlines of the late 1950s on Boar Lane would see a marked rise during the following decade when Mary Quant's influence came to bear. But, before then it was largely billowing skirts and flouncing petticoats that were the order of the day. On this obviously bright and sunny day, the Direct Raincoat Company would have been having a thin time of it, but our northern weather meant that not too many days would pass before the heavens opened and trade picked up again. As well as the traditional raincoat, there were also handy Pac-a-macs that could be rolled up to fit in your pocket. Other similar styles included transparent plastic coats, topped off with the ubiquitous rainhood. The Singer sewing shop was popular because most women were in the habit of making some of their own clothes, running up a pair of curtains or kitting out the children

thanks to their housewifery skills. Sewing machines were in use in the mid-19th century, but were somewhat impractical as the circular movement of the shuttle took a twist out of the thread at every revolution. In 1850, Isaac Merritt Singer (1811-75) invented the first machine that used a needle that travelled in a straight line and delivered the thread in a vertical motion. He also replaced the hand crank with a foot treadle to give his machine the basic design that would last until modern times. Electric motors, first seen as early as 1880, speeded up things for the better off, but the principle of Singer's first model has held good.

Below left: This wartime photograph of Briggate was taken in the early 1940s. Dixons offered 'service with a smile'. There was not much to laugh about, however, during those worrying times. For a long time we seemed to be standing alone against the threat of the Nazi jackboot that had stamped its way across Europe, thrown our lads out of France via Dunkirk and supported the Luftwaffe as it rained death and destruction from the skies in nightly bombing raids on our major industrial centres and historic towns. Rationing of even the basics meant we had to tighten our belts, which was easier said than done because coupons were needed for those as well. The Cash Clothing Company was one of the cheaper outlets where many locals found that their limited resources might stretch a little further. The Stylo shoe shop that suggested we 'step out in style' was ever hopeful, despite the fact that most people found it difficult to keep up with

modern fashion trends whilst huddled in an Anderson shelter or heading off to the factory in support of the war effort. Just to the right is the narrow entrance to the Bay Horse Hotel, where a plaque now stands denoting this on the modernised and pedestrianised Briggate of today.

Below: It was a chilly February day on Briggate in 1944. The northwest side of the street shows the corner of Parker's Hotel on the left, with Wren's Hotel, these days The Wrens at 56-61 New Briggate. The latter was a handy watering role near to Merrion Street. It was a favourite of those visiting the Civic Playhouse, now the Civic Theatre, that was established in the former Mechanics' Institute. Rothwell's furniture store can be seen to the right. This part of the city has seen one of the biggest transformations anywhere in Leeds during the latter years of the 20th century. It is still part of the heartland of city centre shopping, but its face has been dramatically changed, particularly with the introduction of pedestrianisation. However, thankfully, it has not been ruined by the sort of town planners who blighted so many other places in the country with their robotic designs for uniform shopping centres. Redevelopment from the 1980s saw much of historic Briggate that had survived earlier changes being renovated rather than replaced. Thornton's Arcade and Queen's Arcade benefited from this sympathetic approach and regained something of their original atmosphere. Victoria Street got its lovely glass roof in 1990 and the shop fronts are largely in keeping with the Edwardian style that Frank Matcham envisaged. This leading architect was also responsible for such fine architecture as the Blackpool Opera House, London Palladium and Glasgow's Theatre Royal.

EVENTS OF THE 1940s

WHAT'S ON?

In wartime Britain few families were without a wireless set. It was the most popular form of entertainment, and programmes such as ITMA, Music While You Work and Workers' Playtime provided the people with an escape from the harsh realities of bombing raids and ration books. In 1946 the BBC introduced the Light Programme, the Home Service and the Third Programme, which gave audiences a wider choice of listening.

GETTING AROUND

October 1948 saw the production of Britain's first new car designs since before the war. The Morris Minor was destined for fame as one of the most popular family cars, while the four-wheel-drive Land Rover answered the need for a British-made off-road vehicle.

The country was deeply in the red, however, because of overseas debts incurred during the war. The post-war export drive that followed meant that British drivers had a long wait for their own new car.

SPORTING CHANCE

American World Heavyweight Boxing Champion Joe Louis, who first took the title back in 1937, ruled the world of boxing during the 1930s and 40s, making a name for himself as unbeatable. Time after time he successfully defended his title against all comers, finally retiring in 1948 after fighting an amazing 25 title bouts throughout his boxing career. Louis died in 1981 at the age of 67.

The Saxone shoe shop stood on the corner of Briggate with Duncan Street and Boar Lane, along which the Bedford lorry was heading towards the camera. Saxone has a long tradition, dating back to 1783 when shoes were hand made. Kilmarnock was the original centre for the business that eventually metamorphosised in 1901 into the Saxone we know today. It was the offspring of a marriage of two different but related activities, the manufacture and the selling of shoes. It retained its dual character, which proved its trend and is one of the reasons why it continued to flourish in a world that had grown much more competitive than it was at the start of the last century. There are many young children who took their first steps in a pair of Jumping Jacks bought at the store that boasted 'no foot too difficult to fit'. Careful scrutiny of the road markings outside the shop gives a clue that this was a scene from 1943. The white flashes and edgings on kerbstones at the street corners were there to help traffic move safely during the blackout. Even with a reduction in the number of vehicles on the road and the use of such markings, night time movement was fraught with difficulty and a little danger. Many was the bump and scrape in these conditions, with a few more serious collisions for good measure as drivers peered through the gloom trying to get their bearings.

EVENTS & OCCASIONS

Left: The royal motorcade passed the Brotherton Wing of Leeds General Infirmary during the Queen and the Duke of Edinburgh's 1958 visit. It is easily the city's oldest hospital, with a history reaching back to June 1767 when a group of gentlemen met to discuss the provision of medical care for the sick and needy. Temporary premises were found on Kirkgate as the search began for a site for a purpose-built Infirmary. An appropriate place was chosen on ground next to the Coloured Cloth Hall, now the site of the Post Office in City Square. The foundation stone of the first General Infirmary was laid on 10th October 1768 by Edwin Lascelles, later Lord Harewood, one of the earliest benefactors. The red brick, stone-faced two storey building opened in March 1771, with just 27 beds. By 1785 there was room for 100 inpatients and the infirmary had already established a reputaion for being one of the best in England. As the town's population increased, it was decided to rebuild the hospital on a new site on Great George Street, then known as the Sunny Bank Estate. The new Infirmary was opened in May 1868 by the Prince of Wales, later King Edward VII. Various extensions followed that included the Brotherton wing built to house private patients. As the royals passed underneath, nurses and patients waved from every vantage point possible.

Above: On a damp and miserable 2nd June 1953, Queen Elizabeth II was crowned in Westminster Abbey. The weather had little effect on the national celebrations that were held as the whole country took to the streets to mark the occasion with street parties, carnivals and general festivities. Some of us watched the event on flickering black and white television screens. Colour broadcasting was not available until the late 1960s. Only a minority had its 'goggle box', so the majority who wished to see moving images of the event had to wait until the following day when footage was rushed to the cinemas. The News Theatre on City Square was one of those cinemas dedicated to providing film of important events and general day to day stories that are now covered by television magazine and news programmes. Pathé, with its logo of the crowing cock, was one of the most influential companies specialising in newsreels. They were produced from 1910 until mid 1956. At first, they were silent with title cards mentioning the action on the screen. Voice-over narration was added in the early 1930s. The company was founded in France in 1895 by Charles Pathé. In Britain, the main competition for this branch of the film industry came from Movietone, the first to introduce sound. It produced newsreels from 1929to 1969.

Above: The page boy got rather carried away and was in danger of leaving the carnival queen trailing in his wake until a helping hand halted his progress. Deidre Blackburn, the 13-year old who had the honour that many of her pals would have killed for, led her attendants in the procession in front of the Quarry Hill flats. No doubt, though pleased to be part of the parade, they would have given their eyeteeth to be in Deidre's shoes. The estate's carnival was an annual event and this one in 1950, like so many of the others, began with the procession and continued throughout the day with a host of activities until late in the evening. By now, young Deidre will probably be a long retired granny, but she will surely have photographic memories of the day that she was the centre of attention carefully kept in an album that she brings out from time to time. The home where she lived was built to a design idea that was successfully used on the Karl Marx Hof flats in Vienna. Architect RAH Livett also visited an estate at Cité de la Muett at Drancy in France to investigate the revolutionary new building technique used there. However, Quarry Hill was never properly finished as it had few shops and no community hall. Social problems and vandalism bedevilled it in the 1960s and it was demolished in 1978.

Below: Something special has obviously caught this little girl's attention during the fancy dress competition at the 1951 Quarry Hill Carnival. With her ribboned hair, pretty pinafore dress and ankle socks she was every inch of what a kiddie should be. Totally engrossed in the entertainment, her youthful innocence is a sheer joy to behold. In the 21st century she might already be made up to look like a mini adult or be relaxing in front of a DVD or computer game. This photograph displays the essence of what people envisaged when the Quarry Hill estate was designed. It was to be the essence of community living, an extension of the family life on our back streets in the 1930s when everyone knew one another and gran lived just around the corner. Quarry Hill is one of the earliest inhabited parts of Leeds. Extensive building work took place here in the 1780s, providing back-to-back housing. By the 1830s, though, overcrowding led to insanitary condition which, in turn, gave rise to disease and high mortality rates. It became so bad that in 1910 a decision was made to clear the slums. New building work eventually gave us the Quarry Hill flats that got their first residents in 1938. It was the largest housing scheme in the country at the time and aimed to incorporate the latest housing ideas and techniques.

Below: The motorcade bowling along The Headrow attracted thousands to turn out along the route. Excited people craned their necks to get a better view and cheered loudly as the royal visitors passed by. Children waving little flags on sticks and large Union flags hanging from balconies and windows marked the importance of the occasion. Some even ran along behind the rows of onlookers in an effort to maintain a view for as long as possible. In 1958 the crowds were noisy, but well behaved. Police controlling the ranks of loyal subjects had an easy job as no-one was foolish or ill mannered enough to break out of the lines. Interest in the royal family was high and it was long before the days when apathy and antagonism towards the monarchy would affect a number of the population. Queen Elizabeth II, accompanied by the faithful Duke of Edinburgh, was greeted by civic dignitaries at the Town Hall. Interest in the royals was at a high and seeing them in the flesh always attracted a great display of affection. In years gone by, these important personages were quite remote, but the increasing popularity of television brought them closer to the general public. The Carling and Wright shop saw a huge upsurge in sales around the time of the Queen's coronation in 1953. Many bought their sets just to be able to witness that memorable event in Westminster Abbey.

Right: The Quarry Hill Tenants' Association was founded in 1946 and continued to be the umbrella group for focussing the council's attention on matters that were problematic on the estate or to individual residents. It also organised an annual carnival that was rounded off by a children's party at St James' Hall. The first of these was held in 1947 and became a popular feature until the last one in 1962 when the Association was wound up. In this 1952 example, the newly crowned carnival Queen looked thrilled with the honour that had been given to her. In the background, one of the boys watching the ceremony looks distinctly unimpressed as he obviously wished to be off somewhere else practising his leg glances or cover drives. The Queen's attendants had scrubbed up well for the morning. No doubt insults about looking like dogs' dinners had been bandied about, but they seem pleased enough as they faced the

camera. In their teenage years they would hide away the family album or blush with embarrassment when a pictorial record of the only day in their lives when they had clean faces and neatly parted hair was brought out. By now, as men collecting their bus passes for the first time, they will have regained a sense of pride that they were singled out for attention.

Below left: Quarry Hill flats were a steel frame and concrete clad construction. It was heralded as state of the art council housing when the first residents moved in just before the start of the second world war. Built eight storeys high, there was a total of 938 units that, at their peak, accommodated over 3,000 people. High rise was seen to be the future for low cost housing, a view that continued long into the second half of the 20th century. The Quarry Hill complex was eventually to prove

to be a disastrous concept. Design faults, corrosion and costly repairs, allied with social problems, led to tenants being rehoused in the 1970s. Before then, the estate had enjoyed some happy times. Many tenants were happy to have somewhere warm, dry and clean in which to live because the majority had experience of the slum properties that lacked many of the basic necessities. For quite a while, there was a happy community spirit, best demonstrated by the annual carnival. In 1951, the

year of the Festival of Britain, it was 14 year old Alma Brown's turn to carry the Queen's bouquet. She lived in Oastler House and is seen here flanked by her attendants, Mollie Evers and Pat Wilkinson. Alma was a pupil at Roseville Secondary Modern. This was one of the schools that formed part of the new system of education for 11-15 year olds after the war. At the age of 11 children sat tests in English, arithmetic and intelligence that determined if they were academic enough to go to a grammar school. If not, the secondary modern beckoned.

Below: The winner of the fancy dress competition in the 1948 Quarry Hill Carnival used the theme of 'that's what little girls are made of' as the inspiration for her costume. Doubtlessly, mum had worked hard sewing the various sugar and spice elements onto her dress and she got her reward when her daughter was presented with the silver cup. The judges decided that she stood out among the various Indian princesses, hula girls, chefs, Bo Peeps, flower girls and soldiers who paraded by. One of the competitors who failed to make it into the prizes adopted a period costume with the witty slogan 'A famous Leeds poisonality' hanging on a card around her neck. She was dressed as Mary Bateman, 'The Yorkshire Witch', hanged in 1809 for a series of grisly poisionings. Her body was dissected in public to raise funds for the Infirmary and her skeleton is now kept in the Thackery Medical Museum. The judges obviously preferred twee representations rather than a mixture of wit and horror. We can safely presume that the bobby in the background was a real one and not a rather tall nine year old entrant! Quarry Hill flats can be seen in the background. Aimed to incorporate the latest housing ideas and techniques, the flats had solid fuel ranges, electric lighting, a state of the art refuse disposal system and communal facilities.

TRANSPORT

The Standard Life Assurance Building dominated this corner of City Square in the 1930s. The view from the Royal Exchange into Infirmary Street shows that, even three quarters of a century ago, this was a very busy part of the city. One car driver can be seen chancing his luck by executing a right turn in front of the No 2 tram bearing down upon him. It is going to be a tight squeeze and no wonder that the chap with the horse and cart is giving him a quizzical stare. As well as this obstacle, it would seem that our feckless driver has not spotted the small saloon sneaking up on the inside of the tram. Let us hope that disaster was avoided, but it must have been a close shave neverthe-less. This sort of driving was common at the time. Considering the comparatively light number of road users, compared with today, accident statistics made frightening reading. In 1931, there were 22 fatalities per day on our roads. This was a remarkable figure when we look at current levels. There are now 15 times as many vehicles on the move, but deaths have been reduced by half. In comparative terms, that is a 30 fold reduction. It was no surprise that the Ministry of Transport introduced its advisory booklet, the 'Highway Code', in 1931, nor that it started to legislate for pedestrian crossings, more traffic lights, use of dipped headlights and the driving test.

Above: The shelters on the traffic island in City Square, with the imposing presence of the Queen's hotel behind, provided a modicum of relief from the elements for passengers waiting to board a tram to take them home after a day's shopping. They gave only limited protection when the rain drove in or the wind whistled through the open bars on the structures. They had gone through worse privations in the war, so a little discomfort hardly compared. In the 1950s, everybody found it difficult to get back to normal during those austere years. Immediately after the war, the country voted in a new government that it hoped would take it into the second half of the century with renewed vigour. It was to be disappointed and turned back to the old guard in 1951 when Winston Churchill reappeared at 10 Downing Street. His best days, though, were well behind him and it was not until the coming of Harold Macmillan, 'Supermac' to the cartoonists, that Britain could measure an upward swing. By the end of the decade, the economy was booming once again and we looked forward to a much brighter future. The early 1950s had been a painful transition from hostilities to happiness, but we got there. Even our soccer club got back into Division One in 1956 and the county cricket team won the championship as the decade ended.

Below: This sight of City Square in the early 1930s shows a horse and cart as well as a handcart being employed as a contrast to the modern trams, cars and motor buses that are also pictured. The old days were still clinging on, but new times were fast seeing the back of horse power and Shanks's pony. It was all change in Leeds during the early 20th century. The population had grown to 178,000, according to the 1901 census. City Square was created and the Black Prince and eight nymphs arrived to decorate it in 1903. The following year saw the founding of the university, the building of St Anne's RC Cathedral and the opening of the new city market. Electrification of the trams, the opening of the first cinema and the introduction of motorbuses all meant that we were entering modern and exciting times. In the early 20th century the main industries were engineering and tailoring. As the century unfolded, the importance of manufacturing industry declined and, instead, service industries grew rapidly. Some of the people in this photograph would have benefited from living in the new council houses that were built in the 1920s. They might also have been grateful for treatment at St James' Hospital, founded in 1925.

Below: At one time it seemed that all the cars on the roads were of a uniform hue. Even motor manufacturer Henry Ford said that customers could have any colour they liked, as long as it was black. By the mid-1950s, a few different shades were on offer, as we can see from this picture of Wellington Street where the Whingate tram was passing James Hare's serge manufacturing business. Established in 1865, the company was originally a merchant and manufacturer of woollens and worsteds for the men's and ladies' tailoring trade. Even in those early days it was clear that the founder recognised that good customer relations and reliable service backed up by constantly striving for higher standards of quality were the chief ingredients of building a successful business. The company extended greatly in the earlier part of the 20th century, establishing other areas of trading including a silk department. This was to provide the business with a new impetus as the demand for traditional textiles fell. In 1983, the business started to specialise in silks, becoming one of the largest worldwide distributors of such fabrics. By the time James Hare's descendants had moved into silk, there were countless colours and shades used to paint motor cars, many with outlandishly exotic names. In the early 2000s, grey or silver had become the most popular choice.

Above: April 1954, on Boar Lane looking towards City Square, has a hint of the problems of road congestion that was to become an increasing problem for every town and city centre, and one we have not solved over half of a century later. Lorries, buses, trams and cars all dodged in and out as they jockeyed for position. For those on long-haul journeys, there were no motorways and bypasses were few and far between. Quite often, the only way from A to B necessitated crossing a major centre, adding to the volume of local traffic that was already beginning to become a headache. The cross-Pennine link was a major consideration for many years. Even as far back as the 1930s, discussion was taking place on the need for a fast road route between Lancashire and Yorkshire. It was eventually agreed that it would be an extension of the East Lancashire Road, but little positive action was taken before the war, except for the reservation of land for the future construction of an all-purpose road, then known as the Yorkshire Branch Road. It was not until 1961 that the Ministry of Transport invited the County Councils of Lancashire and the West Riding to survey and recommend a route for a motorway. The stretch between Eccles and Outlane, Huddersfield was inaugurated in 1971, though it would be several more years before it was extended further into Yorkshire.

AT WORK

Below: Victory in Europe was celebrated in style in May 1945. Every street, municipal building and workplace was draped in Union flags and bunting in a show of national pride. The joyous celebrations were also tinged with a touch of relief that the terrible days that stretched back for nearly six years were now a thing of the past. These factory girls might have paused for a monent to think what peacetime meant for them and others of their sex. About the only benefit that the war had brought to them was the one of full employment. With their husbands and fathers away at the front, women were actively encouraged to take up jobs that had traditionally been performed by men. They drove lorries, worked in heavy engineering industries, operated specialist machinery, harvested the crops and organised the offices. This level of responsibility and sense of purpose, not to mention the wage packet, was something that many would be reluctant to relinquish when the time came. It caused friction in some households when men returned home and expected the women to go back to being housewives. Women's lib is something we think of as a 1970s' movement, but there was an equivalent a quarter of a century earlier. Men who had been away a long time often found that they could not adjust to the way their wives now thought and friction resulted in more marriage breakdowns than had ever been seen before.

Top right: This was state of the art architecture, or so our parents and grandparents were led to believe. Pictured in 1939, not long after the first families moved in, Quarry Hill was meant to be almost self sufficient. When fully completed, there were to be shops, a community centre, swimming pool, playgrounds and open spaces where people, used to overcrowded slums, could relish a little bit of openness. There was a laundry equipped with up to date dryers and even a mortuary with a laying out room. The

demolished in 1978. The West Yorkshire Playhouse and Quarry House now occupy the site.

Left: Taken in 1934, this is the skeleton of the Quarry Hill flats project. Prefabricated concrete would be added later to the steel framework. The design and construction of the flats was an ambitious project first used on the Continent. After World War I, Prime Minister David Lloyd George promised Britons that he would oversee the rebuilding of a country that would mean 'homes fit for heroes'. Certainly, much of the accommodation our members of the armed forces were used to before they joined up was substandard. Refurbishment of older properties and any new building work had, of need, been put on hold during that war. Consequently, the overcrowding and insanitary conditions in the poorer districts of large towns and cities became an even more acute problem. At the start of the century, the life expectancy of a new born boy was a miserable 45 years. Of course vaccines and medicines were limited in their scope and medical knowledge was underdeveloped. Penicillin would not become available for more than 30 years. Marry these factors with the living conditions of the poor and it is little wonder that the mortality rate, especially among infants, was so high. By the 1930s, albeit much later than the government promised, cities such as Liverpool, London and Manchester had begun to sweep away many of the Victorian slums and replace them with new council houses and flats. Leeds soon followed suit.

flats varied in the number of rooms they had, but an average home had two or three bedrooms, a living room, bathroom and kitchen. The latter opened onto a balcony that had a coalhole and window box. Gas and electricity were laid on, in addition to the fireplaces for solid fuel. Many families coming into Quarry Hill had never had the luxury of a fitted bath and indoor toilet. Each flat had an outlet for radio that was relayed throughout the complex. The onset of the second world war meant that some of the originally planned features and facilities were never completed. The sense of community was at its best in the immediate postwar years, but by the 1960s attitudes had begun to change and the decline in the estate began. Tenants were rehoused from 1973 and the flats

A Harrison (Bedding) Ltd - Over a century of bed manufacturing

The Leeds-based firm of A Harrison (Bedding) Limited has a distinguished history reaching back over more than a century. The family company is one of Yorkshire's oldest bedding firms.

The company's roots can be traced back to at least 1886 when the firm was listed in the Leeds Directory in the Trades section under the heading Bedstead, Bedding & Mattress Manufacturers and trading as Spink & Edgar.

Arthur Spink, who had previously worked for Joseph Longley, a bed manufacturer in Leeds, had started the business. He recruited John Edgar as a salesman and called the new firm Spink & Edgar. They set up in business at 60 Carlton Cross Street off Woodhouse Lane. This was the area which saw the subsequent arrival of William Rhodes, who started as a flock merchant in Birstall. Gradually Rhodes' firm evolved into Somnus Bedding which took over a number of small firms in and around Carlton Street and became a dominant firm in the industry for more than 70 years.

By 1889 the firm Spink & Edgar had come to be known as Spink & Co. Arthur Spink had been joined in the business by his two younger brothers, Charles Spink on sales and John Spink as master mattress maker. The

Top left: Albert Harrison, 1947.
Below: The company's premises in Wade Lane.

firm had by then moved to new premises situated at Belgrave Terrace in Belgrave Street, off North Street, Leeds.

The business continued to expand to such an extent that it was possible to bring in two young apprentices, Albert Harrison and Albert Parker, who apparently met while one was pushing the company hand-cart. They were both to play a significant part in the company's history.

Moving again, to premises at Wade Lane in Leeds, the firm began operating as a ticking supplier and bed maker as well as a bedstead and wire mattress maker.

Always moving forwards on a path of continual expansion and development new premises were found in the Richmond Hill area and a factory was opened there to manufacture wire mattresses, an activity which would continue until the mid-1950s.

At Richmond Hill the company was managed by Albert Harrison. Deliveries were still made by hand-cart, mainly to the centre of the Leeds furniture world situated at St Peter's Square near the Parish Church. However, the firm also delivered to the numerous street corner pawnshops all around the city suburbs.

It was at some point during the 1920s that a new type of mattress was introduced. The mattress had a spring interior and proved to be a resounding success. Until then however the bulk of sales had been in mattresses consisting of wool, horsehair, feather and straw for use on solid wood bedsteads with wire frames made to last a lifetime.

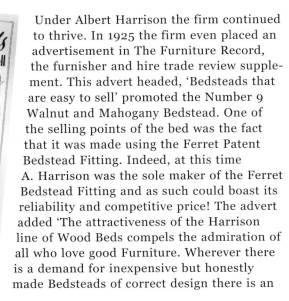

Under Albert Harrison the firm continued to thrive. In 1925 the firm even placed an advertisement in The Furniture Record, the furnisher and hire trade review supplement. This advert headed, 'Bedsteads that are easy to sell' promoted the Number 9 Walnut and Mahogany Bedstead. One of the selling points of the bed was the fact that it was made using the Ferret Patent Bedstead Fitting. Indeed, at this time A. Harrison was the sole maker of the Ferret Bedstead Fitting and as such could boast its reliability and competitive price! The advert added 'The attractiveness of the Harrison line of Wood Beds compels the admiration of all who love good Furniture. Wherever there is a demand for inexpensive but honestly made Bedsteads of correct design there is an

Top: An early company van.
Above: An advertisement Albert Harrison placed in The Furniture Record in 1925.

ever increased sale for Harrison's products...'

It was partly due to these confident advertisements that the firm managed to sell so many of its products. One buyer of a Harrison bed that year was a Mr Nicholson of St Michael's Lane, Leeds. A company invoice from 1925, still preserved, states that Mr Nicholson's purchase cost him £4/6/0d. Included in this price was a 4ft 6in wire mattress with flock, a feather bolster, a pillow and Ferret fittings.

Increased sales led to the inclusion of Harrison's in The Furniture Record of 1926. In an article entitled, 'Wholesale Enterprise in Yorkshire', the firm is grouped with other businesses as, 'leading Wholesalers and Manufacturers connected with the Furnishing and Allied Trades'. The article explained how the firms were coping with the after effects of the General Strike. A. Harrison had only 50 per cent power supply which was a significant handicap to the firm during an extremely busy period.

It was this increased workload that led to the firm being incorporated as a Limited Company in 1933. That important year was also marked by the emergence of Albert Parker as an equal partner in the company. Before then Albert had gathered experience working as a master mattress maker for other

prestigious bed companies including, Somnus, Wheeler and, earlier, Spink and Co.

Albert wanted a stake in the company so much that, to fund his investment he sold coal to the local residents from a horse and cart in the evenings. His hard work paid off. When Albert Harrison finally retired in 1937, Albert Parker carried the business forward himself.

The second world war, like the first, had taken its toll on British industry. A. Harrison did not escape wholly unscathed: the firm experienced a levelling off in its previous rapid growth but was not badly affected in any other way.

The firm contributed to the war effort making hospital mattresses and palliasses for the forces. During the post war years the business expanded: this was accomplished partly due to the flexibility of the

management who worked on the shop floor when the order book was full and the firm was busy, or visited customers to drum up trade when business was slack.

During this time the retail showrooms at Wade Lane did good business and

Top: A 1925 invoice to a Mr Nicholson of St Michael's Lane, Leeds.
Above right: Ron Spinks.
Right: Mrs Dorothy Spinks, mother of Peter Spinks and van driver Malcolm Squires who was with the firm from the age of fourteen until retiring at sixty five.

remained open until 1947. In 1949 Leslie Parker, Albert's son, joined the firm.

In 1950 A. Harrison was able to acquire its second van, the first company vehicle, having been bought from Tates of Leeds in 1934. Also in 1950 Albert Parker's son-in-law Ron Spinks, who had married Dorothy Parker in 1939, joined the firm.
It was also during the early 1950s that the firm was awarded a BSI Standard, allowing it to guarantee its mattress fillings for five years. Sadly in 1952 Albert Harrison died. Nevertheless, his name still lives on in the title of the firm he helped to build.

In 1958 the company moved from its Richmond Hill premises to a 10,000 sq. ft. site at Croft Square, Hunslet Road. This move took the company into premises previously occupied by its competitors, Wheelers, where Albert Parker had made mattresses in his youth.

By this time the business was effectively being run by Ron Spinks and Leslie Parker, Ron taking charge of sales and Leslie controlling production. Albert Parker was however understandably reluctant to let go of the reins and so everything was still done under his close scrutiny.

By the 1960s the business was thriving once again and the firm needed to move to larger premises. A suitable site was found by coming to an arrangement with spring manufacturer, Siddall and Hilton, in that, for the 18,000 sq ft of Hawthorne Mill, Lower Wortly, Harrisons would take springs exclusively from S & H.

Harrisons moved in 1963 and, at a grand opening the Deputy Lord Mayor of Leeds, Councillor S Symmonds, cut the ribbon on a new £30,000 extension and trade showroom for the company at Hawthorne Mill. The opening was also commemorated with special thanks being given to the firm's employees who had all played a part in the firm's success. In fact, the Deputy Lord Mayor made several presentations to employees for long service.

In 1964, Peter Spinks, the company's current Chairman joined the firm. The expansions completed during the late 1960s and early 1970s were mainly in order to cope with the firm's growing contract business. Ron Spinks took over the management of the contract side of the business and amongst the contracts that the firm managed to secure were specialist

Top: *The Somnus factory in Carlton Cross Street.*
Left: *An early Somnus delivery vehicle.*

work for local authorities, hospitals, universities and boarding schools. Another important development was the setting up of an export side of the business in the shape of services to the US Forces in both America and Europe.

The firm's Chairman, Leslie Parker, retired in 1977 after 28 years with the company. To celebrate his retirement, the firm made a presentation to Leslie and a picture of the event was printed in the local newspaper showing Leslie reclining on one of the firm's beds with the caption, 'Uncle puts his feet up'! On his retirement, Leslie handed over the company to Peter Spinks who also took over the management of the domestic and general side of the business.

In 1979 A Harrison (Bedding) Limited moved from Hawthorne Mill to a 38, 000 sq ft factory situated in Westland Road. From there Peter Spinks moved the focus of the company from the contract side of the business to retail trade. With the use of display stands

and other point of sale materials the professionalism of the operation was increased as Harrisons moved into the luxury quality bed market.

Another generation of the Spinks family joined the firm in 1987 when Peter's son, Simon Spinks, started

Right: *A Somnus Tufting Press, 1933.*
Below: *Somnus Spring Shop in 1933.*

work. By 1989, partly due to the development of pocket springs, the firm had become so successful that the factory production in a day was actually equal to a month's production during the pre-war years.

In 1991 the firm's success continued with a move to the second (58,000 sq ft) factory in Westland Road. From there the company's reputation was further enhanced when the first Revolution Spring Bed was introduced using the Revolution Spring system developed by Harrisons. In 1999 new extensions were added to the factory increasing the site to 77,000 sq. ft. Innovations included the new patented Revolution spring. The new 'spring-within-a-spring' system, awarded Millennium Product status by the Design Council, and attracted the attention of the world's biggest spring maker, which bought the rights to manufacture and sell it outside the UK.

In 2001 Harrison acquired the prestigious Somnus trade name from the Vi Spring company. By then that business was already more than eighty years old having roots going back to 1840 when William Rhodes began making fillings for cushions, pillows and mattresses at Carr Mills in Birstall. In subsequent decades the firm, now making its own mattresses and pillows, moved to Batley, Birkenshaw and, in 1905, to Carlton Cross Mills off Woodhouse Lane in Leeds. In the late 1960s following a move to a new factory on the West Park ring road the firm was taken over by Slumberland, which in turn amalgamated with Vi Spring in 1970 under the Duport group. A year later the Leeds factory closed at which point Harrison was able to take on key members of the Somnus manufacturing staff.

Top: New spring machines.
Right: Simon, Daniel and Peter Spinks.

Today, with Peter Spinks as Chairman, Simon as Managing Director, and a thoroughly professional management and workforce, the Harrison Group continues to thrive. There is also a new generation, Daniel Harrison Spinks, waiting in the wings. The firm has evolved into a Group with Harrison Beds and the Spink & Edgar name now synonymous with the finest beds money can buy. The Group's subsidiary firm is a Corporate Member of the Guild of Master Craftsmen and continues to produce some of the world's finest hand crafted beds delivered to everyone from royalty to aristocracy, including customers such as Boris Yeltsin and the occupants of 11 Downing Street!

In 2005 the Westland Road factory was extended yet again to over 100,000 sq ft after purchasing the next-door premises.

Should the company's founders to step into the firm's factory today they would not recognise the technology and materials now used. Despite this however, they would find no change in the dedication, skill and attention to detail that is still an integral part of the company's success. It is these attributes that will undoubtedly ensure a second century of success from the Harrison Group.

The company has seen its most vigorous growth in the last 15 years. Today their customers include the John Lewis Partnership, Harrods, Feather & Black as well as many high quality independents. The future of bed making in Leeds is very good. It is these attributes that will undoubtedly ensure the second century of manufacturing top quality bed products through the Harrison Group: Somnus, Spink & Edgar, Harrison Beds and NuBed.

Should any reader have additional information on the history of A Harrison (Bedding) Ltd or Somnus, would they please contact Mr Peter Spinks on 0113 2055200 who would be most interested to hear from them.

Evans of Leeds - A genius for property

One thing which can be said for Leeds is that it never seems to stand still. In recent times new buildings and other developments have arisen everywhere, from the White Rose Shopping Centre to countless other changes to the cityscape. And Leeds is far from being unique in this. From one end of Britain to the other enterprise, innovation and prosperity have combined to create one of the most dynamic periods in British history, a period matched only by the Victorian building boom.

The driving force behind the spectacular changes seen all across the country has most frequently been a group of farsighted property developers who have seized the opportunity to create a new 21st century environment.

And amongst the largest, oldest and most prestigious of those property developers is Evans of Leeds.

In 2006 the Evans Property Group, one of Britain's longest-established and best-known property companies, significantly strengthened its board amidst plans to double the size of its asset base over the next five years. The Leeds-based company, chaired by Michael Evans, invited to join as non-executives, Ian Henderson, the former chief executive of Land Securities, the UK's biggest quoted property company; Ian Marcus, the head of the European Real Estate Investment Banking Group at Credit Suisse; John Stephen, chairman of the English business of Jones Lang LaSalle, one of the world's biggest real estate consultants and Peter Wilbraham, a partner at

Cobbetts, one of the leading planning lawyers in the North of England.

But what were the origins of this enormously influential and innovative family business?

The headquarters of Evans of Leeds was opened by the Lord Mayor of Leeds Councillor JL Carter in April 1990.

The opening of that flagship building at Millshaw on the Leeds Ring Road marked fifty years of progress and growth for one of the north's leading property companies.

It is now almost seventy years since Fred Evans created the company that in his lifetime would control property throughout the country and claim as its tenants some of the top companies in British industry and commerce. By the late 1990s, following the company founder's death, the group of investment

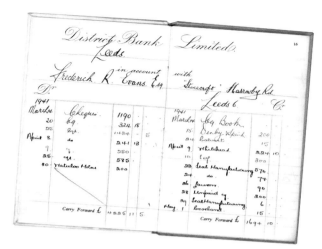

companies would hold assets of more than £300 million and its shareholders' funds exceed £181 million.

Frederick Redvers Evans to give him his full name was proudly named by his patriotic parents after General Sir Redvers Buller who had led the British Army during the Boer War. Fred Evans was an Army boxing champion during his own military service in the first world war. In peacetime he began his own transport business after buying his own delivery vehicle from the widow of a former friend: in addition to carrying out house furniture removals he also transported furniture from manufacturers in London to retailers in Leeds.

The business began in Waterloo Street in a single-storey building, which would subsequently become part of the Tetley complex. Later a move was made to Waterloo Mills, Waterloo Lane in Bramley.

Fred Evans was an optimist. In those interwar years anyone in business certainly had to be. The generation which experienced the 1920's and 1930's is now fading away; the times were however some of the hardest ever experienced in Britain for both individuals and businesses alike. Only an optimist with an unlimited capacity for hard work and an exceptional gift for spotting opportunities could create a successful business.

Though the Waterloo theme was continued with the firm's Telegraphic address which was simply 'Waterloo Leeds' Fred Evans was not about to meet his own Waterloo in business terms – quite the contrary.

Left: Hunslet Mills, (former blanket mill) Goodman Street, Leeds 10. Top: A company bank book from the Second World War.

The roots of the Evans group go back to those pre-second world war days in south Leeds when Fred Evans began to build up a thriving plant hire business. During the war the company was involved in plant hire and civil engineering. Much of the plant was used in the construction of airfields and in open cast coal mining.

After the second world war Fred began to acquire some astutely purchased sites, mainly redundant wartime airfields, to form the basis of the present property portfolio.

Some house building was done by the company in the 1940's and 1950's with a partner named Eric Scott, and together they built the Southleigh Estate off Dewsbury Road.

The late 1950's was a remarkable period. Business optimism and prosperity had returned after a generation of austerity. Prime Minster Harold Macmillan famously said that people had never had it so good – and it was true.

By 1962 Fred Evans knew the company needed larger headquarters if it was to make further progress. He obtained temporary planning permission and built his new headquarters on a former open cast coal site at Millshaw on the outskirts of Leeds which he had bought from Farnley Estates. Permanent planning permission was granted many years later. It was a fine example of his foresight. The open countryside that surrounded the spot became one of the major commercial areas of the city's suburbs where premises would be keenly sought by many major companies.

That first headquarters building was a functional two-storey design typical of the early 1960's. By 1969 however FR Evans (Leeds) Ltd had outgrown the

Top: *A letterhead from 1964.*
Right: *Millshaw headquarters in 1964.*

premises so a second building was constructed connected to the first by a bridge and designed in an architectural style less likely to become dated.

In 1971 under the guidance and direction of Fred's son Michael Evans the family floated the company on the stock market. They employed the services of Hambros Bank and solicitors Travers Smith Braithwaite. Cecil Berens, a director of Hambros, became the company's first chairman.

After the flotation of the company it continued to invest in industrial property. Subsequently however it was decided to alter the balance of the portfolio and include commercial and retail investments. Soon even the enlarged Millshaw headquarters were hard pressed to cope with the increasing size of the group. Inevitably a decision was taken to rebuild the headquarters yet again. This time the style would be classical, a building which would add a good deal of dignity to an area of Leeds already graced by the premises of major banks and other prestigious organisations.

For much of the period following flotation the company was in the extremely competent hands of Ernest Curtis and George Best. George Best died in 1994 and was sorely missed at the company's silver jubilee celebrations. He played a most important part in steering the company in its relentless drive for rent roll growth. Ernest Curtis remained a non-executive member of the Board, offering his wisdom and experience.

The management team is now headed by John Bell who joined the company in 1994 from Yorkshire Water. The policies so strongly advocated by George Best were still followed and by the late

1990's rental income stood in excess of £29 million a year. The company had a cautious and modest development programme in which the majority of its properties were pre-let, each contributing to capital growth.

Fred Evans died in 1992, leaving the company in the capable hands of his family, whose members still remain its principle shareholders, providing stability and continuity and enabling the company to make long-term plans unaffected by short-term considerations.

The Group continued to expand, by 1998 it was employing a staff of 65 under the direction of the main board which was then chaired by John Padovan. Michael Evans was Vice-Chairman and his three sons Roderick, Andreas and Dominic were by now also members of the Board.

Evans of Leeds PLC, as the company was known during its listing on the London Stock Exchange, had been floated in 1971 with assets of less than £8m and an annual rent roll of around £700,000. Since its flotation the Company reported increased profits each and every year and for almost a quarter of century, dividend growth was 10% p.a. This was an enviable record matched by few companies in the property development sector. Following the introduction of new accounting regulations which detrimentally affected its share price, the effect of which would be felt for many years, it was decided, in 1999, to de-list the company. John Bell commented recently: 'The decision to de-list gave us the freedom to answer only to ourselves'.

Since then the business has bloomed – both metaphorically and literally.

In 2001, the first year the company entered the Leeds in Bloom competition, it won the Shield not only for the overall best premises but also the best newcomer award. Evans of Leeds won the shield three years running and thereafter has won first place in the category and also the Floral Cup. In 2006 the judges again awarded the company the Gold prize for the best gardens in the city-wide large business premises category.

Meanwhile 2001, the year Evans of Leeds began saying it with flowers, saw the inception of a new and refreshing approach to property in the form of Evans Easyspace Limited. The original concept has since been modified slightly but the basic tenet of providing offices and workshops to the 'SME' small and medium sized enterprises market on flexible terms, giving Easy-In Easy-Out options has remained the same. Whilst the company no longer solely owns Evans Easyspace Limited, it still has an interest in it and has been retained as asset manager. The business has a gross

value of £115m with 1,200 units developed and plans to grow its portfolio to £300m in the next 3-5 years.

In 2006, for the second year running the Evans Property Group has been voted Property Company of the Year for Yorkshire and the North East in the Estates Gazette annual awards. The accolade for the privately owned property investment and development company, whose work stretches from Scotland to the south, followed another year of record financial performance, in which profits before tax exceeded £30m for the first time. Managing Director, John Bell, said: 'We see the award as the icing on the cake and find it particularly gratifying because it was decided on votes from our peers throughout the property industry'. With its investment portfolio of over £650m Evans is one of the UK's largest private property companies.

The numbers are quite staggering. Net asset value has risen by over £250m since going private. The company owns 80 addresses which are occupied by over 700

The total value of the current development programme is in excess of £750 million which will provide a source of prime stock for the Evans portfolio at a time when it can not be sourced in the open market.

Most recent of the firm's initiatives has been the development of Evans Business Living. This is another new concept in office provision, launched in 2006. By creating small offices for the owner-occupier market, the company feels it is neatly plugging a gap in the market.

The company will continue to follow the business strategy which has served it so well in the past. The quality of its rent roll, the strength of its balance sheet, the development potential of its existing sites, the prospect of its joint venture companies and the success of the White Rose Shopping Centre should enable it to maintain steady progress in the years ahead.

companies. Pre-tax profits to March 2006 was £32.5million, a 58% improvement on the previous 12 months. Current gross assets are in the region of £657m, with a rent roll of £35million.

Amongst the company's key schemes currently underway are 300 acres at Fradley Park, Staffordshire which has consent for over 4 million sq ft of industrial property. The company has already completed over 1.6 million sq ft and a 700,000 sq. ft. distribution warehouse is being planned.

In central Rotherham an office development is proposed on 14 acres, a key part of the regeneration of this Yorkshire town, which the company plans to redevelop as 500,000 sq ft of offices and some community facilities.

In York 720 flats within the city walls at Hungate are being built in partnership with Crosby Homes and Land Securities. In addition the company has a further eight schemes in progress with planning consent for over 2,000 units.

A 132-bedroom 'Dakota Hotel' development project is managed by an Evans' subsidiary.

For the next few years Evans Property Group intends to concentrate on its substantial development programme rather than look for new acquisitions. Opportunities overseas may also begin to appear on its radar: but as and when it does venture overseas, it will be on its terms and done the Evans way.

Whatever the future holds one thing is certain: those who work for Evans of Leeds today can never forget the firm's Yorkshire roots, nor the debt they owe to company founder, the extraordinary Fred Evans OBE.

Left: *An aerial view of Millshaw in 1969.*
Top: *The proposed office development on 14 acres in central Rotherham.* ***Right:*** *The award winning Evans headquarters, 2006.*

Sanderson Weatherall - Surveying the past

Noted for its high level of director involvement and personal service, today Sanderson Weatherall is ranked amongst Britain's Top 25 surveying firms. It is the largest such firm in Leeds.

Declared Property Adviser of the Year for the North East & Yorkshire at the Estates Gazette Awards for two years running in 2005 and 2006, the award gave public recognition to the quality of work being provided by the firm and also the high degree of satisfaction expressed by its clients.

The firm's early days can be traced back as far as 1833 to Thomas Hardwick. Thomas had begun his working life as a drysalter but his enterprising and ambitious spirit had led him to take the bold and ambitious step of setting up his own business. The earliest known record of the company is that of a poster dated in this year, advertising the firm's existence as an estate agent.

Whilst the Thomas Hardwick firm was busy developing and trading as an estate agent, another business that was to play a significant part in the history of Sanderson Weatherall was established. In 1843 Joshua Bramham also took the decision to form his own business, but in contrast to Thomas, Joshua set up a rent collecting organisation.

Throughout the mid to late 19th century Thomas Hardwick developed, in the process taking on different partners, and accordingly changed names several times. In 1845 Thomas was joined in business by Winter Hardwick and the firm became known as, Thomas and Winter Hardwick. A year later the firm was reformed again as Hardwick and Best, and in 1867 another partner, George Tute Young, joined the business which became, Hardwick, Best and Young.

Joshua Bramham had also taken on a partner in his business by 1870. Walter Gale joined the firm which consequently became, Bramham and Gale. With Walter on board the business developed into an active commercial concern. Up until the 1969 amalgamation with Thomas Hardwick's company, Bramham and Gale was probably the main firm involved in both residential and commercial property management in the city of Leeds.

The next significant landmark in the company's history came in 1876. That year Walter D Hollis, an agricultural auctioneer from Garforth, joined Hardwick, Best and Young and the firm was reformed once again, this time as Hardwick Young and Walter D Hollis. During this period of the company's history the business only extended as far as the tramway system and the emphasis had turned to furniture and chattel valuation and sales.

When George Tute Young, the senior partner, died his son-in-law, Stenson Webb, was taken into partnership by Walter Hollis, so carrying on the family connection.

Walter Hollis retired in 1909. Ten years later his protégé, Stenson Webb died. Bernard Webb took over the running of the firm along with J W Shepherd. Later in 1919 Walter Hollis' son, Arthur who was an assistant in the business, joined the other men as a partner though the firm continued to be known as Hollis and Webb.

The flourishing business managed to emerge from the first world war intact and throughout the inter-war years operated from premises situated at 3 Park Place. The building was primitive and the open fires meant that it was impossible to keep the office clean. There was a large furniture warehouse at ground level and two sales rooms on the first floor, one for chattels and one for property. At this time the accounting was still done by hand, the telephones and typewriters were rather rudimentary and as well as the trams, buses and trains, the business also used Shank's Pony.

The firm expanded its activities into commercial and agricultural property during the 1930s. In 1935 Hollis and Webb managed the Earl of Halifax's estate, the 3,000 acre Temple Newsome estate, near Leeds. The firm has maintained its involvement with successive Earls of Halifax to this day.

In 1939, Arthur Hollis was joined as partner by Nigel Richardson who had been with the firm since 1927. It was also at around this date that another Richardson, Stanley Richardson, joined the firm as an office boy. Arthur Hollis proved to be one of the great provincial agents either side of the second world war, and from 1943 to 1944 he was appointed President of the Auctioneers Institute.

At the war's end in 1945, Hollis and Webb and Bramham and Gale both became active in commercial property. Hollis and Webb expanded into management and

Bramham and Gale expanded into development and agency work.

The property development boom of the 1960s saw the commercial business becoming increasingly important and consequently, the furniture sales operation was closed. When Arthur Hollis retired in 1961, Nigel Richardson was the sole remaining partner and he was joined briefly by Arthur's sons, Geoffrey and Christopher. Finally, in 1964, the firm was able to move from Park Place to CMA House at the corner of King Street. This move marked the end of chattel sales and valuations and led to the amalgamation of Hollis and Webb with Bramham and Gale in 1969 to form, Hollis Webb and Gale.

Far left: The company's earliest record of existence.
Below: Caressa House Estate sold by Weatherall Green and Smith in the 1950s.

The amalgamated firm had expanded to eight partners by 1971, including Gordon Brown and David Richardson, and was involved in property development, agency and investment work. Two years later, Hollis Webb and Gale amalgamated again, this time with another long established national firm, Weatherall Green and Smith. That year, 1973, also saw the two remaining members of the original families, Holton Gale and Nigel Richardson retiring from the business after over 45 years service each.

David Yorke and Gordon Brown became senior partners and led the company through the property crash of the mid-1970s and the recessions of the 1980s. Yet the firm was so successful that in 1980 it was able to open a plant

Above: Brendan Foody, Former Chairman of Weatherall Green and Smith. **Right and below:** *Apsley House, Wellington Street, fully refurbished in the late 1990s and let by Weatherall Green and Smith.*

and machinery department which became an important aspect for its many commercial and industrial clients.

This concentration meant that the residential sales operations were closed down and commercial property became the focus. Specialist departments were opened in building consultancy, rating, plant auctions and corporate recovery advice. By the mid 1980s turnover exceeded £1 million for the first time.

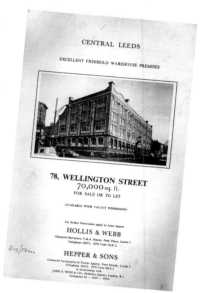

The firm celebrated 150 years in business in 1983. By then it had developed into an international company with four main European offices in Leeds, Paris, Frankfurt and New York and had also developed a flourishing regional practice of chartered surveyors.

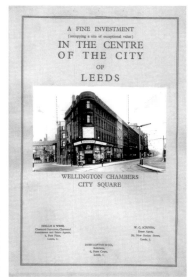

Green & Smith was to merge with Sanderson Townend & Gilbert to form today's Sanderson Weatherall. This merger extended the group office network to include Newcastle, Teesside and London and made it into one of the largest practices in Leeds and Newcastle. Thereafter the company began to extend its influence into a national practice, developing services in London for existing clients as well as Northern based clients who had property interests in the South.

Embarking upon the 1990s under the name Weatherall Green and Smith, during the decade the firm's clients became more internationally based. The firm remained independent but experienced several changes. In 1991, an office was established in Manchester which developed into a profitable force in the local market.

The year 1999 was an important one in the history of the firm in which several new developments took place, increasing and expanding the company's sphere of influence. Weatherall Green and Smith was incorporated as a limited company and four new shareholder directors were appointed to the firm. The firm made the decision to make the Leeds and Manchester offices a separate limited company within the Weatheralls' Group.

Over the next four years, the company extended its professional work, and developed town planning and project management as specialisms in Leeds and Manchester

In 2003 the firm acquired plant and machinery valuers, Singletons of Manchester. They moved into the Manchester premises and developed what became a significant P&M practice across the North of England. Three months later it was announced that Weatherall

The size of the company nearly doubled, and turnover at the point of merger was £11.8m, reaching nearly £18m in 2006. Small niche practices have been acquired, for example rating specialists Dixon Rankin, which enlarged the London presence.

Brendan Foody, who had led the firm in recent years, retired in October 2004. Today, led by Peter Dunlop, who has been Managing Director of the firm since the merger in 2003, expansion by way of both acquisition and organic growth is set to continue for the foreseeable future.

Top left and top right: *The former Wellington Chambers, City Square.* **Left:** *Peter Dunlop, Managing Director.*

Gateways School - Traditional values for the 21st century

E ducation has always been the key to a successful life, and because of that fact those who have found success in life invariably look back to 'the happiest days of their lives' and give due credit to the academic institutions which helped forge their characters.

Gateways is a forward-thinking, highly successful school for girls aged 3 to 18, and for boys aged 3 to 7, situated in the village of Harewood, just north of Leeds and within easy reach of Harrogate, Wetherby and the surrounding villages. The school occupies the former Dower House of the Harewood Estate. In recent times the house has been carefully restored and refurbished to fully reveal its many fine and original architectural features.

Founded in 1941 as an independent day nursery and preparatory school for girls and boys, Gateways has been controlled by a non-profit making educational trust since

1961, and now offers a full range of education from the age of three years up to university entrance.

Pupils attend each day, and are drawn not only from the city of Leeds but also from towns and villages such as Boston Spa, Harrogate, Ilkley, Otley and Wetherby.

But what were the origins of this exceptional educational establishment?

It might seem impossible for two middle aged teachers without funds in the midst of the second world war to bring a school into being, but that is exactly what the school's founders, Miss Nancye Simpson and Miss Lilian Cox, achieved.

*Top: The Porch area of the School. **Above right:** The Dower House showing The Winter Garden. **Right:** The School at Alwoodley.*

Miss Simpson supplied the determination, Miss Cox the dynamic enthusiasm. The one without the other might never have succeeded.

Both Miss Simpson and Miss Cox were teaching in the junior school of Roundhay High when war broke out in September 1939. It soon became apparent to them that parents in the professions and in business were reluctant to send their children away from home in wartime and that there was support for a school of the kind they longed to open.

With the help of a few supporters, not least the MP Sir Charles Davies, the pair were able to acquire a house: 15 Sandmoor Avenue, Alwoodley with suitably large rooms and – there was a war on – an air raid shelter in the grounds. It didn't take the two teachers long to choose the name Gateways and the open gate design for the school badge.

The school opened in September 1941 with just 15 pupils. By the second term there were 30 pupils attending each day.

Pupil numbers soon increased until inevitably more space was needed. When in 1947 the chance came to lease the Dower House in Harewood Miss Simpson and Miss Cox took it eagerly, helped by advice from Mr Ronald Schofield, foreshadowing the role he was to play for so long as mentor and supporter of the school.

The new building had many large light rooms, 13 acres of land, a view over fields and woods yet was on the main

Top: An art class in The Winter Garden.
Above right: A letter from Queen Mary thanking the School and congratulating the children on their work.
Right: An old classroom.

road and bus route. Accommodation for the now 80 pupils was ideal.

Both Miss Simpson and Miss Cox were determined that their pupils should have an all-round education, which should include especially art and music. Miss Simpson was gifted in both; after she eventually left Gateways she held a one-woman show of her paintings in Paris.

Miss Simpson became Lady Wort in 1955 when she left the school on marrying Sir Alfred Wort, High Court Judge for India. One of the legacies she left behind however was her love of art – something acknowledged even in royal circles when examples of the pupils' work were later sent to Queen Mary.

Dear Miss Cox,

Very many thanks to you and the staff and pupils of Gateways for the delightful 'card' you have sent me. It has given me very great pleasure and the drawings of Harewood House and the lino-cuts are all excellent, and I would be very grateful if you would congratulate the children and your Art Mistress and thank them for the very evident trouble that has been taken to make the drawings correct in every detail.

My best wishes to you all for 1961.

Yours sincerely

Mary.

Miss Cox was now the sole Headmistress, a role she would fill until 1963 when she retired due to poor health.

Lilian Cox had been born in London in 1898 the daughter of a former blacksmith who had through hard work obtained sufficient education and training to become a Methodist minister. Because of her parents' peripatetic lifestyle, moving every three years, Lilian went to boarding school in Southport. She then went on the London University from where she graduated in 1919 and went straight into teaching. In the mid-1920s Lilian went to India to work in Methodist missions but poor health forced her to return. She came to Leeds and became friends with Nancye Simpson, a friendship which was to lead to the founding of Gateways.

By the time Lilian Cox retired some 200 pupils were attending the school, a degree of growth which Miss Cox could look back upon on with a great deal of justifiable pride and satisfaction.

Lilian Cox loved education. She knew the truth in the statement that education should enable the individual to be able to entertain an idea, to entertain a guest, and to entertain oneself. It was not a question of simply acquiring skills but of appreciating all that life had to offer and learning as much as possible about how to take advantage of it, and most of all making a contribution to society as a result of that learning. For her, education was a spiritual matter rather than merely a commercial transaction.

Growth in the late 1950s came with the development of the High School, an additional form being added each year. Yet when Jean Gardner became headmistress in 1963 there was still no sixth form or Nursery

Department. During the next nine years the school was both 'topped' and 'tailed'. Support came from everyone involved, but especially from Ronald Schofield now Chairman of the Governors. Despite the many calls on his time as the Managing Director of Schofields Department Store he always found time to discuss new plans for the school.

A new Science Laboratory, Language Laboratory, and what would eventually become the Schofield Building, would be the ultimate outcome of Miss Gardner and Mr Schofield's planning and - not least - Ronald Schofield's personal generosity.

As the buildings went up or were adapted, so the academic results climbed and the curriculum widened. Gateways too began to be noticed in the sports arena. The lacrosse team under Mrs Margaret Pickersgill's dedication and discipline reached dizzy heights for what was then still a very small school, taking the Southern Schools' Tournament by storm and making far larger establishments wonder just who these Northerners were.

Top: *The whole School photographed in 1961.*
Above: *Opening of the New Science Block in 1982.*
Left: *Lord Harewood pictured with pupils after opening the new Junior School (Youngers), September 1993.*

Mrs Pickersgill, who had personally planned the school grounds, had been associated with Gateways since 1945 as a parent, history teacher and subsequently deputy headmistress. She retired in 1973, but continued as the school's librarian until 1988 ending an involvement with the school which spanned a remarkable 43 years.

Headmistress Jean Gardner left the school in 1972 to take up another post in Ashford, Middlesex. Her successor, as headmistress was Mary Beard. Mrs Beard would remain in post until her retirement in 1982. The big projects in Mrs Beard's time at the school began with finding crumbling beams in the ancient roof of the Hall and culminated some time later in the transformation of the derelict stable block next to the Hall, creating the fine new Science laboratories, new kitchens and a dining hall. In all of these projects she was supported and encouraged by the Chairman of Governors Mr Victor Watson, who remains the school's longest-standing governor and a great supporter of Gateways.

The successive headships of Leslie Brown, Jenny Stephen, and today's headmistress Denise Davidson, would witness the expansion and development of the school, creating a prestigious girls' school for the 21st Century.

Today the delightful Gateways campus is home to five individual but integrated schools – The Gatehouse Nursery, Littlegates (infants), Youngers (juniors), High School and Sixth Form. More than 200 pupils attend the Preparatory School and over 300 the High School, a far cry from that day in 1941 when just 15 pupils were present for Gateways' opening day.

Within the expansive grounds the original Dower House is still part of the school but fine new buildings have been progressively and sympathetically added. These include the Watson Building used for Art, Design and Technology, The Performing Arts Centre, The Gatehouse Nursery and an impressive Sports Hall in addition to the Cox-Simpson Library and the new Schofield Building which houses the latest technology for Modern Languages and new Science Labs.

Now in the 21st Century the current Governors and Staff are helping the girls of today prepare for exciting futures; but whilst doing so they never forget the past and the vision set out by the school's founders Nancye Simpson and Lilian Cox. For those at Gateways the message of the past to be applied today and in the future is that those who teach should concern themselves to understand and care for the uniqueness of each person attending the school. Many thousands can now look back, as Old Gatewegians, and truthfully declare that their years at Gateways really were the best days of their lives. And many more will do so in the future.

Below left: Jane Tomlinson (left) opening of the Fitness Suite in 2005. Also pictured from left to right are: Mrs Denise Davidson, Headmistress, the Lady Mayoress of Leeds Mrs Patricia Hyde, the Lord Mayor of Leeds Mr William Hyde, Mr Martin Shaw, Chairman of the Governors and Dame Fanny Waterman.
Below: Gateways School today.

Geo Spence - Hardware through hard times

Today Geo. Spence & Sons Ltd based at 105 Wellington Road is Leeds' best-known ironmonger, hardware, hand tools and power tools supplier. The long established family firm also stocks garden tools, industrial clothing, electrical fittings and a range of plumbing fittings.

George Spence, helped by his wife Sarah, started a Leather Merchant business in the late 1880s from a small shop in West Street, Leeds but soon moved to 52 Wellington Road, next to the North Eastern Gas Board's 'Town Gas' plant with its distinctive and all-pervading aroma.

The couple had three sons - Sydney born in 1900, Frederick in 1902 and Rowley in 1906.

Another shop was opened at 55 Beeston Road. The family moved to Beeston Road and lived above the shop, which Sarah ran, whilst George looked after the Wellington Road business.

When he became old enough Sydney worked in the business until he joined the Army to fight in the first world war.

With Sydney away Frederick left school at the age of 14 to help in the business.

When Sydney returned from the war he was never quite the same again: like so many others he may well have been suffering from shell shock. Nevertheless he took over the running of the Beeston shop which he continued to run until it was earmarked for demolition in the late 1960s.

Above: Advertising for leather boot protectors from the 1930s. Below: An early photograph of the Spence family, from left to right: George, Sarah, Sydney, Frederick and Rowley. Right: Geo Spence and Sons Ltd, 52 Wellington Road, 1954. Picture supplied by kind permission of West Yorkshire Archive Service.

Meanwhile, in the early 1920s, the youngest son, Rowley, joined the expanding business. In 1923 plans were approved for alterations and additions to 52 and 54 Wellington Road. The plans included the addition of a second floor above the previously single story buildings. These changes almost doubled the working area.

A hole in the ceiling which was used to hoist leather to the second floor some 14ft up had only had a simple single bar to stop anyone falling through - today a health and safety nightmare!

It was around this time that George invented and began making ' Toppa' metal boot protectors which were sold all over the country (this was a forerunner to the Blakey Segs). A later development was the 'Neeto' leather boot protector which featured on the business' advertising material.

Between the wars Rowley opened a shop at 388-390 Dewsbury Road, but when war broke out once more he worked at Burtonwood, a US airforce base near Warrington in Lancashire.

Frederick continued to run the Wellington Road shop by day, and work at night in the blackout as a volunteer ambulance driver. One of his tasks was collecting the wounded from Leeds railway station and taking them on to local hospitals.

The firm did its bit for the war effort making articles for the American Air Force. Because of their knowledge of leatherwork they were asked to make protective gaiters (spats) for use in Flying Fortress aircraft. The company had a Ministry licence to obtain the specially treated freeze-proof leather required.

Some of this work was done in the workshop at Wellington Road, however George, now living with Fred and his wife Ivah in Hetton Road, and in his seventies, worked on the dining room table punching the lacing holes.

George, then 75, now decided to hand the business over to his sons.

After the war there was a great deal of change. The shoe repair trade dwindled and the firm had to adapt. They began to develop the tool supply side of the business.

In 1951 the business became a limited company - Geo. Spence and Sons Ltd.

The decade saw a gradual diversification into ironmongery, batteries, torches etc., followed by the addition of DIY-related products.

During the 1950s and 60s the company had an established van delivery round covering Leeds and the surrounding towns, servicing the shoe repairing trade. Several Bedford Dormobiles were used over the years

Expansion saw the shop area extended by knocking through and incorporating the ground floor of number 54 Wellington Road - previously the butchers shop of James William Wilson.

In the mid 1950s Fredericks son-in-law, Alan Ball, joined the company. One of the first jobs he did was to build a shelving area with a walkway in the new area of number 54. This allowed easy access to the higher shelves without the use of a ladder which was the case in number 52.

In 1961 Frederick's son Terence, then aged 16, joined the company as a junior straight from school after completing his RSA exams.

Terry remembers as a small boy on many occasions when visiting 52 that Fred would stand him on the platform of the leather scale and weigh him with a set of cast iron weights.

With the rising interest in DIY now came the introduction of hardboard, plywood, beadings and the like.

Right: Frederick Spence in 1960.
Below: Geo Spence and Sons Ltd, Wellington Road in August 1977. Pictured are Alan Ball (left) and Fred Myers.

The fashion for 'flushing' doors made sheets of hardboard and the matching beading a major seller. Along with this people were also fitting ball catches and pull handles to doors. Pearl-effect handles became the fashion in door furniture and hundreds were sold.

Paraffin heaters were popular too. The company had a 600-gallon tank installed at the back of number 54 for paraffin which was both sold in the shop and delivered.

In the early 1960s the company knocked through into number 56 - formerly J P Keogh shoe repairer. The

company now occupied the whole block between Renton Street and Langham Street including a couple of cottages in Langham Street which were attached to the back of number 56 and used to store of bulky items such as bags of sand and cement.

Fred, Alan and Terry saw the firm through into the 1980s. Fred was

Managing Director: his wife Ivah did all the business administration. Alan was Manager and ran the day to day business

Sydney continued to run his shop in Beeston Road until it was earmarked for demolition in the late 1960s. All though this was a separate business it was supported with help from the family at Wellington Road.

In 1977 the company, now with eight employees, moved into new premises built at 105 Wellington Road. The land and properties around 52 being compulsory purchased for the building of the Armley Gyratory road system.

By then the leather and grindery side of the business had all but died out and at the new premises only stick-on soles, laces and polishes were sold: even this ended within a few years.

The move to 105 meant a better show room area to display a range of woodworking machines. There were regular demonstration days so customers could see the machines in action.

The shelving and storage equipment side of the business grew apace. The firm even shipped a small unit to a customer who had gone to live in New York.

Throughout this time however the mainstay of the business was hand tool and ironmongery sales.

In the 1980s Alan was instrumental in introducing the company's first computerised accounting machine: an Olivetti the size of a desk and incorporating the latest twin 8" floppy disk drives. Pauline Flockton, Terry's sister-in-law, was the first operator on the Sales Ledger, while Barbara, Terry's wife, ran the Purchase Ledger.

During this time Fred gradually reduced his involvement in the day to day running of the business and Barbara took over the paperwork.

By the late 1980s machinery sales had declined somewhat. At this time a member of staff who had been involved with the machinery turned to theft. It was only at the company year-end that the thefts were discovered which caused a financial hiccup. The individual was sacked and the decision was taken to run down the machinery range.

In 1988 Alan started to reduce his working hours as he began to semi-retire. Fred continued to work part-time until only a month before his death in June 1990 at the age of 88.

Alan decided to retire completely in 1993 when he was 65. At this time Barbara became a Director.

Nicholas, Barbara and Terry's son, worked for the company for a short while after university and redesigned the company logo and promotional material.

During the decade shelving sales declined but cordless power tools changed the power tool market and created new opportunities.

In the spring of 2000 a mezzanine floor was installed across the back of the building giving an additional 80 square metres of storage space.

Nick Rose joined the company in 2000 as a sales person and was eventually appointed manager; in 2005 Managing Director Terry reduced his working week to 4 days with Barbara continuing as Director in charge of payroll, accounts and financial matters.

As for the future, with no end in sight for DIY, the Spence name is destined to go on for many more years yet to come.

Top left: *Barbara Spence, Nick Rose and Terry Spence.*
Below: *Geo Spence & Sons Ltd's premises at 105 Wellington Road.*

Hall & Botterill - A cast of millions

Established in 1946, today Hall & Botterill Ltd of Meanwood Road Leeds manufactures a comprehensive range of rainwater hopper heads and gutters, many of which are based on original Victorian and Edwardian designs.

Handmade cast aluminium hoppers are made to complement the company's cast, aluminium rainwater systems and suit round, square and rectangular down pipes.

The range extends from small simple designs to large heavy-duty ornamental hoppers. Decorative motifs, dates and emblems can be incorporated on many of the designs. The range of rainwater hopper heads can be supplied in natural aluminium finish or polyester powder coated in a range of colours.

Below: *Co-founder Mr Eric Botterill pictured left .*
Right: *An early company cheque.*

Reproduction and new designs can be made to order according to customer requirements.

In its ornamental work, the traditions of the firm are jealously maintained; the greatest of care being taken in the making of patterns to ensure that its castings are 'sharp, clean, and full of character'.

The company was established in 1946, the year after the end of the second world war by Mr Eric Botterill and Mr Hall and remains an independent family-owned cast aluminium foundry business.

the foundry as 'Big Betsy' which was for use in power stations.

Mr Eric Botterill was both Chairman and Managing Director of the firm from its inception in September 1946 until his retirement in April 1987 when his daughter Barbra became Chairman whilst Alastair 'Alex' Paterson was appointed Managing Director.

Taking up his appointment on April Fools Day Mr Alex Paterson faced no easy task. In the 1980s the general collapse of the United Kingdom's engineering base was taking its toll of the company. Alex's job was to turn around what was then the company's bleak outlook.

Both Mr Eric Botterill and a Mr Hall had worked at Leyland Foundries on Sayner Lane in Leeds during the war. Mr Eric Botterill was one of the foremost experts in aluminium casting. During the war Rolls Royce was experiencing immense difficulties in casting the Spitfire carburettor: it was Mr Eric Botterill who solved the problem and eliminated the hold up in the production of Spitfire fighter planes.

The company began its life with just three employees from premises in Great George Street before moving to Meanwood Road in 1953.

Using his vast experience Mr Eric Botterill built a foundry employing more than 60 men making power station components for Reyrolle, switchgear components for Ferranti, printing components for Vickers and Crabtrees, Jacquard loom beams for Crabtrees. The company became, and still is, the largest manufacturer of commercial 'body corner' castings. The largest aluminium die casting in the world was cast at Hall & Botterill's, at the time known in

The fact that the company operated from an old run-down mill meant that complying with an avalanche of Health & Safety, employment and building regulations that spewed forth from both Government and from Brussels sapped time, energy and money during a very difficult restructuring process.

Until 1989 the company's main production was sand casting with only a little gravity die-casting. In a complete about-turn the company now abandoned sand casting altogether and switched exclusively to gravity die-casting.

Top and right: *At the time of these pictures, 1960s, Big Betsy was the largest gravity die cast in the world.*

One story in particular illustrates perfectly the company's technical flair, its will to succeed where others struggle and its independent outlook.

Another company had been working for 18 months with an unlimited budget trying to make some castings for petrol tankers. Unhappily the company was having to scrap nine out of ten of its castings because of 'porosity'.

Porosity of cast components – gas bubbles trapped inside them can have a significant impact on the strength of aluminium castings and great care must be taken to minimise the entrapment of gas during casting.

A drinking friend of the buyer suggested that he go and speak with Mr Alex Paterson at Hall & Botterill who was said to 'know a bit about die casting'.

Top: A Crabtree printing machine. Inside were sheet conveyor drums which were sand cast in one piece. ***Above right:*** The one piece sheet conveyor drum after casting. ***Far right:*** The Casting Shop.

The buyer arrived at Meanwood Road leaving the offending gravity die on the back of his wagon. As luck would have it Alex Paterson walked in past the wagon and took a brief look at the die before going in to meet the buyer.

The buyer explained his problem, and that none of the experts in several foundries he had visited could solve the porosity in the castings.

Mr Alex Paterson told the buyer it would cost £600 and two weeks to solve his difficulties. The buyer blew up and asked how Alex could possibly make such a claim when he hadn't even unloaded the die to have a look at it.

Alex explained that just from looking at the die on the way in he had been able to tell which toolmaker had made it. Furthermore in his opinion all the other people who had been asked had looked at the casting and pouring problem with tunnel vision.

The buyer was doubtful but Alex suggested that he left the die with him and if he could not crack the problem he would not charge a penny for the work.

In fact it took only one week for the firm to make alterations to the die and the pouring method. On the buyer's return he was presented with four 'unfettled' castings, exactly as they had been removed from the dies, which were then cut open in front of him using a band saw.

All the castings were porosity-free.

The stunned buyer asked when he could have 200. Alex Paterson simply told him 'Open the boot of your car and we'll put them in now'.

A white-coated clipboard-carrying inspector who had accompanied the buyer now produced a document as thick as a telephone directory and demanded exact details of how the parts were cast and whether the firm met the internationally recognised quality management system standard ISO 9001.

Alex Paterson's response was simply to state that firstly he was happy to fix the die problem for £600 but that he would have to charge millions of pounds for the knowledge that went into that solution: and secondly that the firm did not have ISO 9001 since the company was not prepared to reduce its quality standards for anyone!

Hall & Botterill Ltd fully recognises and appreciates the responsibility of the unique position occupied by its castings in the Trade, and neither effort nor expense is spared in the perfecting of its designs in dies and patterns to ensure the production of only the best quality work.

The company is now setting year on year records in output, with 15 foundry men now using more tonnes of aluminium than when the workforce was 65. Yet remarkably, due to increased technical efficiency, the amount of energy used per tonne in 2006 was only one twentieth of that needed in 1946.

After more than sixty years in the business, today the company is a thriving organisation with a skilled, dedicated and highly motivated work force. It has a well-earned reputation for its product quality, and of nation-wide delivery within 24 hours from receipt of an order. This is achieved by continuous investment and through updating the company's technology, capability and stock of products. Over 1,000,000 castings are currently held. The company is now the largest producer of commercial vehicle corner castings in the UK, and the world's largest range of gravity-die cast aluminium gutters and fittings

A Baldwin & Co - Good foundations

Just like buildings good businesses require good foundations. A lot has changed since 1964 when Arthur Baldwin set up a small building repairs venture founded on a commitment to quality, reliability, efficiency and innovation.

Those whose memories stretch back as far as 1964 will recall a world before colour television: indeed a world which in Britain at least, meant just two television channels – a choice of either BBC or ITV.

In music it was a time when the Beatles and Rolling Stones, then all in their youth, had just come to national prominence. In politics the world was still reeling from the assassination of President Kennedy the previous November in Dallas Texas: in South Africa a little known figure named Nelson Mandela was given a life sentence. In Britain Winston Churchill was still living, though in the last year of his life; the Tory government of Harold Macmillan and Alec Douglas

Home limped to electoral defeat in the shadow of the Profumo Affair. The incoming Labour Prime Minster Harold Wilson famously promised Britons a bright future powered by the 'white-heat of technology'.

And Arthur Baldwin decided to help build that bright future.

What was then a tiny five-man business has grown to become a multi-million pound building industry giant based in Hales Road, off Lower Wortley Lane in Leeds.

Yet the company, today led by Arthur Baldwin's sons, Peter and John, has remained true to its founding principles with customer service at the heart of the Baldwins ethos.

Above: *Peter and John Baldwin.*
Below: *Baldwins' joiners shop.*
Above right: *One of the company's electrical operatives at work.*

Today, in the first decade of the 21st century, Baldwins has nine outlets across the North and is a massive operation specialising in social housing repairs, refurbishment, building maintenance, renovation and new build.

The company has experienced massive growth and enormous success in recent years. Baldwins now has offices in Leeds, Bradford, Rotherham, Harrogate, Teesside and Lancashire, as well as a dozen different divisions – Baldwin Builders, Baldwin Maintenance, AB Joinery, AB Electrical, AB Glazing, AB Plumbing, AB Engineering, AB Drainage, AB Cleaning, AB Plastics, AB Systems and AB Garage Services.

Turnover has been increasing at a remarkable rate, from £42 million in 2005 to over £50 million in 2006.

The company's staff numbers have been increasing just as quickly: the original five has grown to around 600, including 450 skilled and multi-skilled operatives.

All the operatives wear the Baldwin company uniform and carry identity cards. A fully liveried fleet of over 350 service vehicles mobilises and supports the operation and has become an increasingly familiar sight across northern England. In some instances Baldwins has combined its own unique livery with that

of its clients to further demonstrate its commitment to working with, and not just for, its clients.

Every service vehicle is equipped with a standard range of stock items that is replenished every time the vehicle returns to the service centre. The materials stock process is computerised and managed directly by the purchasing and supply chain team based at the head office in Leeds.

Down the years Baldwins has worked closely with a number of major clients, especially Leeds City Council with which it has been a preferred partner since the 1970s. The company has carried out numerous disabled adaptations for the council and competed projects for other departments, including social services, leisure and education.

More recently the advent of the Decent Homes Standard has led to a large volume of refurbishment work for the company: it was selected to work with two of Leeds's 'ALMOs' – Arms Length Management Organisations - Leeds West Homes and Leeds South Homes to deliver repairs to 21,000 properties.

The company has also worked with Bradford City Council on group repair schemes in three of the city's renewal areas. That entailed working on hundreds of homes to renew roof coverings, stone cleaning and pointing and to install new windows and doors amongst other remedial work.

The schemes proved so successful that the company subsequently received requests from a number of other local authorities in South Yorkshire and east Lancashire for a similar service. This is typical, in that much of the work done by Baldwins leads to other contracts following word of mouth recommendation.

Though Baldwins continues to tender for new contracts it always has a solid and satisfied customer base that it can rely on because of its past work.

Baldwins has even worked on a project to provide emergency accommodation for asylum seekers and refugees. In conjunction with a number of local authorities it repaired dilapidated and derelict housing. As the housing was often needed urgently Baldwins had to renovate properties at short notice and as quickly as possible. In many cases it succeeded in renovating and fully furnishing homes in a matter of just days.

The company likes to support local businesses and employs local labour as much as possible. It also

develops training initiatives and provides skills and employment to school leavers – in the form of accredited apprenticeships – and middle-aged employees who want to retrain for the building industry. Baldwins' training road show has visited schools and communities to put forward the construction industry as a career option.

Baldwins has also worked to expand its list of services over the years to include drain clearing, house clearance and commercial cleaning amongst others.

It has also sought to decentralise its operations to locations across northern England wherever they are best placed to meet client needs. This has meant that Baldwins staff reach a wider area and are known throughout the region for the standard of service they provide.

Not a company to let the grass grow under its feet Baldwins is always evaluating ways to improve the range of services it offers to clients. With a firm belief that it is not good enough to be seen as just another contractor doing a fair job, Baldwins is constantly monitoring new developments and innovations to make that vital, meaningful, difference. This policy means offering real innovations that will provide value and benefits to customers, as opposed to mere gimmicks.

Above: *Peter Baldwin being congratulated by Her Majesty the Queen on the successful restoration of the Sun Pavilion (top picture), Harrogate.*

One such innovation that has been developed in-house is the introduction of a real-time hand held technology system that will revolutionise the administration of contracts and produce measurable efficiencies across the board. This will mean a paper-free system that will provide a complete and comprehensive job record including fleet data, routeing information, stock and material requirements and digital photographs. This will allow Baldwins to plan and optimise each operative's daily work schedule.

As well as being available to Baldwins in real time this information can also be made available to the client. Baldwins has already invested heavily in the system and trialled it extensively. It is just a matter of time before it is fully rolled out.

This kind of investment in technology will produce real benefits to clients, tenants and of course Baldwins itself. Introducing a hi-tech computer-driven system to the front line of the building industry is just one of several innovations that Baldwins believes will make a difference and help guarantee a successful future for everyone concerned.

As well as being known for its building work Baldwins has successfully opened new support divisions which dovetail into contracts and enable the company to offer a one stop shop to many clients: these include AB Electrical, AB Drainage, AB Glazing, AB Joinery, AB Metalwork and AB Gas Engineering.

AB Plastic for example was established in 2004 and offers uPVC door and window design, fabrication and installation across northern England from a manufac-

turing unit situated alongside the joinery workshop in Leeds. Also established in 2004 AB Cleaning provides a broad range of tailor-made cleaning services and the clearing of vacant properties including the removal of sharps, fridges and freezer cabinets. AB Systems and Apollo Plant Hire shops compete the Baldwins portfolio.

Baldwins has demonstrated time and again its commitment to broadening its own horizons, modernising and streamlining its services and making itself well placed to move forward in an increasingly demanding and competitive industry.

Yet a rosy future is only possible because of the solidity of the company's foundations.

According to Peter Baldwin: 'Our aim is to treat people as valued customers and look after them in their own homes. Customers today are central to our service as much today as when my father carried out his first building repairs in 1964. Computer systems, streamlining and sustained growth have helped to keep the company up to speed, but it is the company's commitment to good service and our comprehensive manufacturing base that brings clients back to Baldwins time and time again.'

Above: Baldwins' signing a partnership charter with Leeds Homes. *Left:* Before (inset) and after the modernisation to council offices at Huddersfield Civic Centre for Kirklees Council.

Woodhouse Grove School - An all-round education

Founded in 1812 as a boarding school for the sons of Methodist ministers, today Woodhouse Grove School provides a first-class, all-round education for boys and girls, day pupils and boarders alike, from all denominations and from none.

Situated on a 70-acre campus in beautiful parkland at Apperley Bridge between Leeds and Bradford, the school sits in the broad Aire Valley with the dales and moors to the north. Cultural visits, sports fixtures and work experience are easily accessible with Bradford lying to the south, Manchester to the west and Leeds and York to the east.

'The Grove' is one school with three parts, offering continuity of learning from nursery to the threshold of a career. The school's traditional outlook reflects Christian values and forward thinking combined with fine faculties and a splendid environment to provide the best possible education within a strong school community.

The all-round strengths and successes of the senior school are mirrored at Woodhouse Grove's junior school – Brontë House, and its early years department Ashdown Lodge. Whilst at Brontë House small classes, a broad curriculum and excellent extra-curricular activities provide a splendid foundation for children before progressing to The Grove.

In recent years student numbers have grown to 700 in the senior school from age 11, but that number remains small enough for all pupils to be known individually and to make their mark.

The Woodhouse Grove estate was bought for £4,575 in 1811 by the Wesleyan Conference, which was looking for somewhere to open a school for the sons of its preachers. The school opened on 8th January 1812 with just nine pupils.

That year a 35-year old Church of England curate named Patrick visited the school to conduct examinations. During

*Above: The Wesleyan Academy. **Below:** Pupils enjoy a game of cricket in front of the school circa 1900. **Top right:** Dr Vinter (seated centre)and staff pictured in 1912.*

his visit he was introduced to Maria Branwell, the headmaster, John Fannel's niece. The pair married on 29th December 1812 at Guiseley church: their children Charlotte, Emily, Anne and Branwell Brontë would make their family name world famous.

Meanwhile, within five years of its opening, shortage of space almost caused the school to move: happily funds were found to build the necessary extensions.

In the 1820s the school day began at six in the morning and continued until eight when breakfast was served consisting, on five mornings a week, of a piece of dry bread and a small serving of milk. On the other two days breakfast was of porridge and treacle: for dinner there was meat and potatoes. On Sundays corned beef and suet pudding were served.

Even less pleasantly in those far off days, thrashing with a birch rod on bare flesh was the normal punishment for infringement of school rules.

In 1832 a new Chapel was built at a cost of £789. In 1847 a west wing was begun and in 1852 the east wing. At the same time a gas plant was installed on the site of what would later be the Martin Hall in order to provide gas to both the school and to Apperley Bridge railway station.

The school celebrated its Golden Jubilee by erecting a new porch at the front of the school and installing a clock on the east wall of the Schoolroom.

In the 1860s The Grove acquired its first asphalted playground – compensation for no longer being permitted to swim in the Aire because of the increasing industrial pollution in those days.

The specific association with the education of Ministers' sons came to an end in 1883 when it was decided by its Trustees that Woodhouse Grove should be re-established as a 'Lower Middle Class Boarding and Day School.'

Education specifically designed for the offspring of active preachers would continue elsewhere. More than half the pupils left the school leaving just 64 under the new headmaster Dr Arthur Vinter.

Dr Vinter's energetic reign of over 30 years soon saw numbers restored. Under his leadership building work also transformed the school: swimming baths, gymnasium, library and additional dormitory would soon appear.

In 1908 Dr Vinter's Guest Speaker at Prize Day was Viscount Wolverhampton, then a member of Asquith's Liberal Government, who lamented the recent death of another member of the Government, the Attorney General

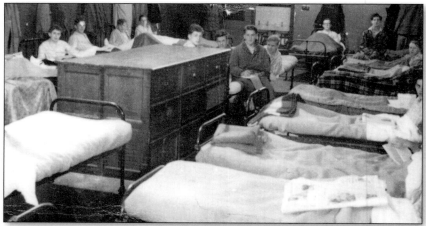

Sir John Lawson Walton: remarkably both were Old Grovians

The Vinter Memorial block was built in 1926.

In 1922 Dr Clifford (Pop) Towlson became Headmaster. Under Dr Towlson the school survived the war, purchased 'Ashdown' in 1934 as a Woodhouse Grove Preparatory School, later renamed Brontë House, and achieved status and standing to join HMC (The Headmaster's Conference).

Dr FC Pritchard succeeded Dr Towlson as Headmaster in 1950, sixteen years earlier he had taken charge at Brontë House at its opening. In the intervening years he had served in the army during the war and had subsequently taught English at Chesterfield Grammar School.

Hillcrest House on the other side of Apperley Lane was bought in 1955 to provide accommodation for a married master and up to a dozen boarders.

In1958 new Chemistry and Physics laboratories were built in a three-storey block on the south side of what would become the Quadrangle. Six years later, on the school's 150th anniversary, the library and gymnasium were linked to the Vinter Memorial building.

By 1972 when David Miller succeeded Dr FC Pritchard as Headmaster there were 384 boys at the school of whom 302 were boarders who still lived under what was still a rather stern, authoritarian and old-fashioned regime.

Over the years however a much more relaxed atmosphere has developed within the school without loss of discipline. Perhaps the natural exuberance of boys has been modified

Woodhouse Grove is an acknowledged centre for sporting excellence. The playing records of its main teams, strong fixture lists, experienced and committed coaches and continued enthusiasm of pupils repeatedly emphasise that reputation for excellence.

Activities available include Athletics, Badminton, Basketball, Cricket, Cross-Country, Dance, Fencing, Football, Golf, Gymnastics, Hockey, Martial Arts, Netball, Physical Fitness, Rounders, Rowing, Rugby, Squash, Swimming and Volleyball.

by the civilising influence of girls being introduced to the school.

Somewhat controversially at the time, girls were allowed to enter the school in 1979. The 'experiment' would prove a great success in promoting and securing the school's reputation as one of England's finest fully co-educational boarding and day schools since 1985.

In recent times over £5,000,000 has been spent on facility development, including a new sports and performing arts centre, new science laboratories, extended ICT facilities, refurbished boarding accommodation, refurbished swimming pool, new junior school hall and much else besides.

Current development projects include a £1.25 million Boarding House to accommodate 44 pupils in en-suite facilities, together with common rooms, lounges and games rooms as well as new staff accommodation. The Sixth Form centre has been refurbished, as has the Library. Plans are underway for a new Music and Drama building with a second Sports Hall to follow.

Although now mainly a day school, during term time the Grove is home to over 120 boarders. The Grove's boarding community keeps the school alive seven days a week and the broader social, national and international mix provided by boarders enriches the whole school.

All pupils however are actively encouraged to take advantage of, and be involved in, as many different activities as possible, both sporting and non-sporting. Activities range from art, computer club and chess through to music and the performing arts.

Top left, facing page: An early schoolroom.
Above left: Boys boarding ready for lights out.
Above: An aerial view of Woodhouse Grove School, 2006.
Right: Headmaster David Humphreys, 2006.

The Grove also has a distinctive voice and sound, and a long tradition of musical excellence provided by the numerous orchestras, bands and ensembles. Classical, jazz, rock and composition are all offered, along with the opportunity to join in with the many choirs and singing groups which enhance many of the school's public occasions.

The numbers of pupils who seize the opportunity to learn and participate enables the school's Director of Music to stage a programme of events at every level of the school.

The new Grove Theatre provides an excellent venue for concerts and musical productions and allows the presentation of a wide repertoire, from informal recitals and instrumental evenings to full choral and orchestral concerts and dramatic productions, giving the audiences an opportunity to fully appreciate the quality and ability of the performers.

Today, under the leadership of Headmaster David Humphreys, Woodhouse Grove is a friendly school with a proud past and an exciting future. The school's fine

academic record speaks for itself. It is a school that offers pupils an all-round education with a wide choice of extracurricular activities to capture their imaginations and channel their energies. The school aims to meet the individual needs of every child, whilst preparing them for the world beyond the classroom - leaving them with a fund of memories which will last a lifetime.

Viamaster Transport Ltd - Kings of the road

Viamaster Transport Ltd was established in 1970 and incorporated on the 20th May 1971: today the Leeds-based firm, based in Elmfield Road, Morley, is still a family owned and family run independent haulage company.

The company specialises in road haulage services for both national and international distribution, and has extensive warehousing facilities services.

From humble beginning in Pudsey Viamaster is now nationally recognised as one of the leading pallet operators in the UK.

Top left and right: *Founders Bernard Warrington and Joan Warrington.* **Below:** *One of Bernard Warrington's first trucks bought to transport sand, gravel and other building materials.*

Now in its fourth decade the company operates from Elmfield Road, Morley, servicing the whole of the UK with its strikingly-liveried fleet of over 60 vehicles.

The firm began life as Viamaster Garages Ltd and was founded by husband and wife team Bernard and Joan Warrington. They operated three vehicles out of a small yard in The Marsh Pudsey, with the office at their home in Waterloo Road, Pudsey, West Yorkshire.

Bernard managed the business and drove one of the vehicles: Joan was company secretary and organised and booked out vehicles. The only other employees were a driver-mechanic and another driver.

Previously Bernard had been an electrician and had started out in business as an electrical contractor wiring new houses. During those years he also built some houses, and bought his first truck for collecting sand and gravel and other building materials. Other builders began asking Bernard to collect for them, leading to Bernard establishing a small transport business, B Warrington & Co, as a sideline, carrying not just building materials but also coal, bales of wool and many other goods.

The haulage side of the firm eventually grew to some 20 vehicles, mainly tipper vehicles, operating alongside the electrical business. By early 1970 however it was clear that the haulage side of the business was being subsidised by the electrical side and it was disposed of. Bernard retained only two flat vehicles with which to start Viamaster Garages Ltd, a small firm which would offer clients a haulage service and vehicle repairs.

Though Bernard could not have known it the opening years of the 1970s were amongst the least propitious in the 20th century for starting any business, let alone one involving road transport. Few haulage firms starting out in this

This page: Two of the company's early vehicles, pictured top is the first of Viamaster's Arctics.

period would survive to see the end of the decade, let alone see in the 21st century.

Inflation which would soon peak at almost 30 per cent would be the least of the transport industry's problems. Far more serious was the Oil Crisis. The crisis began in October 1973 when the Arab oil-producing states decided to simultaneously restrict oil production and raise prices.

Over three months the oil producing countries raised their take on each barrel of oil from $1.75 to $7.00. In a year the price of crude oil imported into Britain rose almost threefold. Inevitably the price of petrol and diesel rose in response.

For many businesses in the transport industry this period was their death knell.

Yet 'when the going gets tough the tough get going'. If Viamaster Transport was going to go down, then it would go down fighting. And Bernard Warrington was not afraid to fight anything that fate might throw at him to keep his fledgling business afloat.

Those firms which did survive the terrible difficulties of the early 1970s found the second half of the decade would reward them for their fortitude and endurance.

In 1979 Bernard and Joan's eldest son Andrew Bernard Warrington joined the business, with younger brother David Kevin Warrington completing the family team in 1987. Both sons would learn the industry at first hand out on the road.

Before joining the firm as a driver Andrew had been an estimator surveyor in the industrial buildings sector. In due course Andrew would progress from driver to

transport manager, through Director and Managing Director, to Chairman and Company Secretary.

David Warrington joined the firm as a driver. His background was similar to his father's: previously he had been an electrician wiring cinemas, fast food outlets and bingo halls. David would progress from driver to Transport Manager and Director before becoming today's Managing and Financial Director.

The company's first significant move had come in 1980 when the business moved from Pudsey to Planetrees Road Laisterdyke in Bradford into a yard and garage unit.

Customers who helped establish Viamaster in its early days included Marshalls of Halifax, Palmers Scaffolding and SGB Scaffolding. The main breakthrough however came in 1982 - a very significant stepping stone for the business - when Viamaster was appointed the carrier for GKN Axles of Kirkstall Forge Leeds, followed by even more extensive haulage contracts from the GKN Kwikform group.

In 1984, with the fleet increased to seven vehicles, the business was on the move again, this time across Bradford to Singleton Street where a warehouse, workshop and yard was leased.

In 1991, with the fleet now increased to 13 vehicles, a freehold haulage depot of some 2.2 acres was bought at Gomersal, Cleckheaton, where the company consolidated its activities with an additional 10,000 sq ft warehouse unit and a yard at Morley.

Top: *Part of the Viamaster fleet in the mid 1990s.*
Right: *Andrew and David Warrington pictured alongside a new Volvo in 1996.*

The company name was simplified in 1996 to Viamaster Transport Ltd; the 'garages' part of the name was dropped because the company no longer carried out vehicle repairs for other parties.

The 4.5 acre site in Elmfield Road, Morley, the firm's present headquarters, was acquired in 1999 to house the growing and substantial fleet of 31 vehicles.

In 2001 the company leased an additional 10,000 sq ft of warehouse at Stourton. Two years later this was increased by an additional 35,000 sq ft warehouse within the same

site to provide a combined total of over 60,000 sq ft storage facility and open areas.

In 2003 Viamaster International Ltd was incorporated offering a freight-forwarding service worldwide to complete the full package. Since Viamaster International Limited was founded it has become highly regarded as one of the major players in 'groupage' and full load services to and from Italy. In addition to its first class Italian operation the company also offers regular departures to and from Spain, complimented by worldwide freight forwarding capabilities by land, sea and air.

Meanwhile Viamaster operates more than 60 vehicles, over 100 trailers and has over 100 employees based in Morley. Vehicles and trailers can be painted and 'decal-ed' in customers' own livery for dedicated contract business.

All vehicles are satellite-tracked to maintain efficiency and regulate environmental issues. The road haulage services are complemented by a warehousing facility of 60,000 sq ft incorporating palletised racking and block stacking. The warehousing division also specialises in receiving and despatching shipping containers and import/export trailers. Viamaster has become what it proudly describes as 'a total logistics provider'.

With the emphasis on service and reliability, the company confidently offers next day services to every United Kingdom postcode. That service ranges from single pallet consignments through to full trailer loads. Besides operating a comprehensive pallet service the company can also accommodate loose-loaded consignments such as cartons, rolls of fabric, and carpets.

Bernard Warrington is now retired, however he remains a director of the company he and his wife founded. Sadly Joan Warrington passed away in 1999 after several years of illness.

Today Andrew and David Warrington run the business along with their wives Anne and Deborah, with the assistance of the third generation of the Warrington family, Andrew's daughter Nicola. Other key personnel include: Mark Ingle, Craig Hirst, Richard Briggs, Ian Davenport Jason Marshall and Joanne Cooper. The senior management team has a wealth of hands-on practical logistical experience capable of meeting the most demanding of customer needs.

Through periods of recession within the UK road haulage services industry, Viamaster Transport Ltd has continued to grow larger and stronger, whilst maintaining the personal touch with its customers.

It has taken four decades to fully establish the business as a leading distribution company within the region: yet the company's steady upward progression is a remarkable example of how significant undertakings can arise from humble beginnings. By a combination of hard work and initiative Viamaster has truly earned its name 'master of the via' – King of the Road.

And what's next? According to the Warrington family 'Our primary aim for the future is to continue to attract new customers by providing the highest levels of service and reliability at all times.'

That sounds like a recipe for an even bigger fleet in the next 40 years!

Top left: *The company's 30,000 sq. ft. 4.5 acre warehouse facility.* **Below:** *One of Viamaster's 60 plus vehicles.*

Lowe Engineering - 70 years on

The name Lowe Engineering – Formally known as George E Lowe Ltd – would have been familiar to those who regularly passed along Kirkstall Road.

The Lowe family began trading in Leeds during the early 1930s, and since then the engineering company they founded has pioneered integrated technical solutions for its multitude of clients across a broad range of critical industrial applications.

Originally the company's focus was on servicing the petrol distribution industry, to which it began supplying storage tanks, pipelines and reconditioned pumps. The 1930s was not the best of times to embark upon a new business. The 'hungry thirties' as the decade became known was a time of terrible poverty arising from the slump in world trade, which had begun in 1929. Despite the Great Depression however some sectors of the economy still continued to move forward, not least the petroleum industry as the internal combustion engine continued to supersede horses and steam power – even if that growth was somewhat slower than it might otherwise have been.

The start of the second world war in 1939 presaged tragedy for individuals; for industry however it was the kick start which the world economy needed. Unemployment ended almost overnight, and the demands of a war economy stimulated both production and innovation to heights never previously achieved. Lowe Engineering, driven by the demands of the 1940s war effort, perfected specialist welding and machining skills in aluminium and steel. After the war that capability enabled the company to further develop and market its own range of products.

During the 1970s integrating that range of equipment into Steam and Water Analysis System Solutions enabled the company to develop an export trade on a global basis, successfully tendering for major new power station projects in India, Hong Kong, China and Africa.

Top: The firm's old Burley Wood Works.
*Left: A Lowe service and maintenance van on route to the power station. **Above:** A steam and water sampling system.*

Through into the 1980s Lowe had become internationally recognised as a leading design authority for a wide range of sample and analysing systems, in applications ranging from power generation to chemical processing plants – spurring dramatic rates of business growth.

In 1987 the company was one of the first in its field to obtain registration under the prestigious ISO 9001 Standard, covering design, manufacture and installation.

Constantly seeking new challenges the company would, in the mid-1990s, further develop its expertise and began to move into environmental monitoring, data capture and reporting systems such as CEMS – Continuous Emissions Monitoring. By the early 21st century it was able to offer the company's own CEMData software - leading-edge computer solutions that complimented its analysis systems. These would include a range of process instruments, 'annunciators' and recorders installed in fully lit, heated and ventilated control cabins.

Following a Management Buy Out completed in 2003 the company restructured, reducing it's large fabrication capability due to competition from Eastern Europe and China, whilst retaining a small niche area. The company

has continued to strengthen and increase its market share within core activities but also provides on-site maintenance and servicing - enabling Lowe Engineering to offer clients a complete package of after-sales solutions and support.

The company has become adept at providing designs for, and working with, local and overseas contractors and end users – many having their own specialised requirements or technical standards, applications, difficulties and, not least, local support for technical and after-sales service. Lowe now has systems working in power plants as far afield as South Africa, India, the Caribbean, the Middle East, SE Asia, Hong Kong and eastern Europe.

Lowe's is a major supplier to the UK power industry, not least Ferrybridge and Drax etc., one of the company's latest and largest projects has been a six-figure contract from Scottish & Southern Energy for an installation at the Peterhead Power Station.

Today the company's management team offers fully integrated solutions to its clients; no matter how big the task it is viewed simply as a new challenge by this always responsive company which prides itself on consistently enhancing its reputation for delivering high standards and quality products.

Top: *New self contained CEMS Laboratories.*
Left and below: *Analysing systems.*

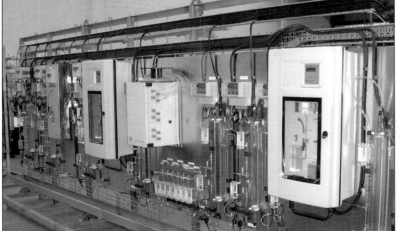

Harold Newsome - A paragon in steel

Harold Newsome Ltd was established in 1937, shortly after Harold Newsome had left a partnership with Edward Bigwood, when both of them decided to form individual businesses of their own. Today the Leeds-based company Harold founded is one of Britain's best-known and well-respected structural engineering firms, specialising in structural steel fabrications.

Harold Newsome was a Master Farrier in the years just before the massive use of motor transportation came to the fore. Eventually however with the phasing out of horse-drawn transport Harold and his staff of five began to specialise in small contract steelwork and structural steelwork for building contractors.

Harold found a plot of land on Elder Road, Bramley which had previously been an old tannery. Harold Newsome Ltd has been based at the same location, the Paragon Works, ever since. In those days there was little labour-saving equipment. The firm's original cranes were hand operated using ropes; steel was moved around on a handcart from the railway sidings.

During the war the company produced components for the famous floating Mulberry Harbours which were towed across the Channel to the coast of Normandy in 1944 in the wake of the D-Day landings.

Harold had two sons, Peter and Geoffrey, who joined the business just after the war. Geoff had been in the mining industry and Peter an RAF officer. After being demobbed Peter began to develop the steel structure business with Geoff.

It was hardly the best of time to join the firm: during the company's lifetime there have been many occasions where the building industry was depressed; yet the firm had always managed to keep going. In 1947 in particular however, there was no work for months because of the 'big freeze': in the end steel had to be dug out of the snow to provide work for the men.

Whilst Peter would spend all his working life with the company, Geoff would eventually concentrate his efforts on an associated business.

Bespoke products are made for each individual project. In the early days all work had to be carried out using templates and, in the absence of calculators, log tables. Large template floors were used with chalk and string lines: in some cases buildings were virtually drawn out full-scale on the floor. Now buildings are designed using computers, far more accurately. Much more complex buildings can be produced, accurate in every detail.

Today the company still remains in family hands. Peter's sons, Paul and Clive Newsome, grandsons of the founder, are joint managing directors.

Paul joined the company on leaving school working as a lowly apprentice, starting at the bottom and working his way up. Clive joined later in 1979 as manager.

Left and top: The Harold Newsome team at work.
Above: A typical example of the modern structures erected by the company.

The site was refurbished in 1980 and a new extension added.

On Peter Newsome's death in the early 1980s his sons took over the firm and continued to develop the structural steel side of the business, incorporating state of the art CAD systems and high tech equipment, producing steel-framed buildings, which are second to none.

Today the company works with most major contractors in the United Kingdom and erects steel-framed buildings throughout the country.

The company has developed steadily from its humble beginnings. Just as Harold Newsome himself changed from being a farrier to become a new kind of specialist in structural steel work, so his successors are not slow to incorporate all the most modern techniques of computer aided design and detailing into their work today.

Seven decades on from its birth, now with 25 full-time staff, Harold Newsome Ltd continues to progress as new methods, materials and techniques are introduced.

Full in-house design facilities mean that the company is exceptionally competitive, and most of its work comes from repeat orders and word of mouth, a testament to the quality of its work and its customers' satisfaction.

The word 'Paragon' means the best. Harold Newsome didn't choose the name of his workplace lightly. And being the best remains the aim of his company to this day.

Clariant - From the Alps to the Pennines

With an annual UK turnover of more than £200m, and a payroll pumping more than £41m into the UK economy in the last few years, speciality chemicals company Clariant is unquestionably a force to be reckoned with.

In the last five years alone, the company, which in the UK is headquartered in Leeds, has invested no less than £24m in the UK, with further investment in the pipeline.

The history of Clariant is directly linked to an event which revolutionised the way we look at the world.

In 1856 a British chemist, Sir William Henry Perkin, was attempting to synthesise the anti-malarial drug quinine from coal tar. During his experiments he accidentally produced a soluble purple dye – the first synthetic dye which it was practical to manufacture on a commercial basis. The colour revolution had begun.

By 1886 the potential of Perkin's discovery had become clear to two innovative Swiss entrepreneurs, chemist Dr Alfred Kern and his partner Edouard Sandoz.

The pair founded the Kern Sandoz Company in Basle, Switzerland and began producing the new coal-tar or 'aniline' dyes at a rate of some 12 tons a year.

From those modest beginnings the company gradually grew and prospered. That growth would one day accelerate as the realisation dawned that synthetic dyes were far from being the only chemicals which could be created using coal tar and other hydrocarbons.

In 1911 the partners decided to expand. The first Sandoz company outside Switzerland was established in the heart

Above: Dr Alfred Kern (left) and Edouard Sandoz.
Below: Laboratory workers in the 1940s.

outstanding service and wide-ranging application know-how make Clariant a preferred partner for its customers. Internationally represented on five continents with over 100 group companies, the Clariant Group employs around 22,500 people. With headquarters in Muttenz near Basle, Switzerland it generated sales of over 8 billion Swiss Francs in 2005.

Clariant's businesses are organised in five divisions: Textile, Leather & Paper Chemicals, Pigments & Additives, Functional Chemicals, Life Science Chemicals and Masterbatches.

of England's wool textile industry in Canal Road, Bradford where it would remain for the next 50 years supplying dyestuffs to the Yorkshire woolen and Lancashire cotton industries. As the Company grew however a move was made to a 48 acre green field site in Calverley Lane, Horsforth near Leeds.

The site, partly hidden in the valley is close to the ring road, and since 1961 has been the base of the Company's UK textiles, leather and paper chemicals division.

The 1990s brought many changes, and on 1st July 1995 the Sandoz Chemicals Division separated from the rest of the Group to become an independent company now known as Clariant.

By 1997 the name Sandoz was destined to disappear completely following the merger of the pharmaceutical and agrochemical business with Ciba to form a new company - Novartis.

That same year, 1997, Clariant in the UK doubled in size through a merger with Hoechst Specialty Chemicals. The former Hoechst businesses were integrated into Clariant strengthening the range and depth of expertise it could offer to its customers.

In 2000, Clariant UK Ltd acquired BTP plc and its group of companies, strengthening even more Clariant's presence as a leading player in the supply of intermediates and active ingredients for the pharmaceutical and agrochemical industries.

The UK company now employs around 350 people at its headquarters in Leeds, and a further 450 people work at seven other Clariant sites in the UK and Eire.

Clariant is a global leader in the field of speciality chemicals. Strong business relationships, commitment to

Clariant is committed to sustainable growth springing from its own innovations. Clariant's innovative products play a key role in its customers' manufacturing and treatment processes or else add value to their end products. The Company's success is based on the know-how of its people and their ability to identify new customer needs at an early stage and to work together with customers to develop innovative, efficient solutions.

With almost a century of experience in West Yorkshire, and a history which goes back to 1886, Clariant's reputation now embraces not just the science of applied chemistry but also such important issues as a concern for the environment.

Continuously reducing the environmental impact of its operations by actively pursuing programmes such as waste and energy minimisation recently led to the company being ranked in the top 50 of Business in the Community's Environment Index for Yorkshire and Humberside.

Above: An aerial view of the company's Horsforth site.
Below: The main reception at the Company's UK Head Office in Leeds.

Redmayne-Bentley - A friend indeed

Back in December 2005 Keith Loudon, Senior Partner in the Leeds-based firm of stockbrokers Redmayne-Bentley, was invited to London to 'push' the button setting off share trading in the UK market. The reason for such an honour was the firm's celebration of an astonishing 130 years in business.

Since the reign of Queen Victoria folk in Leeds have been acquiring shares through the stockbroking firm of Redmayne-Bentley, now based in Merton House on Albion Street.

Equipped with little more than his own coal scuttle and a purchase ledger, it was Christmas 1875 when John Redmayne set up as a stockbroker on his own account at the Leeds Stock Exchange. From that small beginning Redmayne-Bentley has become one of the UK's leading independent private client stockbrokers.

John Redmayne thrived, even when interest in railways declined, because of his overriding passion to provide a first class, highly efficient and above all friendly service to his clients.

Throughout the 20th century able new partners ensured that the firm's reputation flourished. A major landmark was passed in 1965 when Gavin Loudon, Keith Loudon's father, organised the merger of Redmayne & Co with FW Bentley & Co and JW Grainger & Co.

At the time of the 'Big Bang' for the London Stock Exchange in 1986 - which introduced far reaching

A stock exchange was established in Leeds in the mid 19th century because of the Great Railways Boom. John Redmayne's early success was bound up with dealing in railway shares for private investors.

Top: *Senior Partner Keith Loudon setting off share trading in the UK market in December 2005.*
Above right: *A 19th century view of Leeds Stock Exchange.*
Right: *Inside Leeds Stock Exchange in the 1950s.*

on-line share dealing through the Internet - but always with the addition of help and advice for clients who prefer a more personal touch. The firm was also a prime mover in initiating a London Stock Exchange educational campaign to demystify share investment and explain to the public about the long-term benefits of owning shares.

In 2001 the opening of the Redmayne-Bentley Stocks and Shares Shop on Albion Street marked another important development: a first for the firm and a first for Leeds. There, shoppers can have a chat, drink a cup of coffee and buy or sell shares - an echo of Jonathan's Coffee House where the London Stock Market had its origins.

changes to stockbroking in the UK - the Leeds firm had to make some difficult choices. Conventional wisdom dictated that regional firms should join up with others to become large conglomerates, focusing on either the 'top end' of the market, advising wealthy clients, or offer a bargain basement, no frills service to smaller clients. The three partners of Redmayne-Bentley felt differently. They would stay independent by continuing to offer a full range of services to the firm's loyal and growing list of private clients.

The firm's strong Yorkshire roots, its efficient and friendly service, and its expert advice enabled it not just to survive but also to prosper and attract increasing numbers of clients.

Redmayne-Bentley's commission charges were, and would remain, highly competitive. The firm's reputation began to spread across the UK: as it did so, teams of stockbrokers in other parts of the country, attracted by the Redmayne-Bentley style of doing business made approaches asking if they might join up. And so a branch network was born.

As a result of that network Redmayne-Bentley has grown into the UK's leading independent stockbroker with over 30 branches throughout the UK, ranging from the Highlands of Scotland to the South coast.

Despite being proud of its roots and traditions the firm has never been afraid of change, and has often been a leader and innovator. The firm was the first in Leeds to install a teleprinter. It was also one of the first to try out television advertising.

What was true then remains true today: Redmayne-Bentley were amongst the first stockbrokers to introduce

Every year since 1995, when the Investors Chronicle magazine began an annual awards scheme, Redmayne-Bentley has been a consistent award winner: 'Best Regional Broker', 'Best Portfolio manger' and 'Best Innovating Broker' – and not least the coveted top award of 'UK Stockbroker of the Year'.

Though many folk may still be mystified by the world of stocks and shares help is always at hand. And nothing can express that determination to help more eloquently than the uncompromising declaration on Redmayne-Bentley's logo: 'Your Friend on the Stock Exchange'.

Top left: The Dealing Room at Redmayne-Bentley in the 1980s. *Below:* Our friendly brokers always ready to help, Redmayne-Bentley's Stock and Shares shop on Albion Street.

Scattergood & Johnson -
Electrical distributors since 1899

Formed over a century ago in the city of Leeds, Scattergood & Johnson Ltd is today renowned in the electrical engineering distribution industry for its levels of service and customer satisfaction. With nothing but top brand names in stock the company offers its customers more than 40,000 high quality lines at the most competitive prices.

Still privately owned, the company has expanded greatly down the decades. Though once a tiny concern, nowadays Scattergood & Johnson has branches

in Gateshead, Manchester, Glasgow, Sheffield and Walsall, as well as a new head office facility at Lowfields Road in Leeds, built as the platform for the business in its the second hundred years of trading.

The firm of Scattergood & Johnson traces its origins to 1899 and the closing years of Queen Victoria's reign. The business' founder was Bernard P Scattergood who was previously an electrical engineer with Marshall & Fowler. It was four years later when Claude Johnson joined him as a partner. Though Mr Johnson remained with the firm for only two years his name has remained to this day as part of the company title.

In 1912 JN Hargreaves merged his own small business with that of Scattergood & Johnson and the enlarged firm moved to 7-9 Cookridge Street & Alexandra Street. Mr Hargreaves' brother was involved with local collieries, and through him Scattergood & Johnson supplied the

collieries with all their electrical equipment, including the well-known Reyrolle brand plugs and sockets. The firm developed, and was incorporated in 1924 becoming a limited company, at which time JN Hargreaves became managing director.

Three years after the end of the second world war, JN Hargreaves' son, Christopher Hargreaves joined the company after serving a four year electrician's apprenticeship in Peckfield Colliery. Christopher had picked the worst time ever to join the business which was then on the verge of collapse. The company's largest customer had been the collieries, a group of clients which made up nine tenths of the company's sales. In the wake of the nationalisation of the coal industry however its buying practices had changed. Overnight sales at Scattergood & Johnson's plummeted by 90 per cent as its largest customer went elsewhere.

The next five years were an uphill struggle, having to rebuild the business from the ashes of the coal industry nationalisation. In 1953 however the company was appointed English Electric Distributor, providing the cornerstone of a new power and distribution business. The following year Christopher Hargreaves became managing director. The business moved again in 1956, to 30-31 St. Paul's Street, and five years later the company was appointed stockists for MTE Motor Control Gear. Once again they felt the need to move, transporting the business to 37-39 St. Paul's Street a little further along the road, into much bigger premises.

Christopher soon became chairman of the company, gaining complete control, and there followed another move in 1966 to Lowfields Road. Three years later his father died and there followed a period of change, seeing first, Joe Wardell and later, George Beaumont appointed to the board.

In 1982, following a period of good profits and stable trading a branch of Scattergood & Johnson Ltd was opened in Sheffield.

Christopher Hargreaves died in 1987 but the business continued under private ownership. It also continued to thrive. Some of the old franchises were changed in 1999

Facing page, top centre: Scattergood & Johnson's 37-39 St Paul's Street premises. Far left: The company's old Lowfields Road premises. Left: Mr Christopher Hargreaves. Top: Inside the showroom in the 1960s. Right: The company's headoffice, 2006.

and new products were taken on such as Omron Automation and Klockner Moeller Control Gear. Over the millennium the company moved into a new purpose-built head office on Lowfields Road in Leeds. The first year of the new millennium would also see the opening of a new branch in Glasgow, a branch which would be doubled in size in 2001. A new additional warehouse would be opened at the Leeds site in 2002 whilst the final month of that year would witness a move to new purpose built premises in Glasgow. An additional branch of the company would open in Walsall in the Midlands in 2005.

The company has expanded its brief and is now importing directly from the continent and around the world. Products such as Exor touch screens, industrial computers from Italy and Aucom soft starts from New Zealand.

What the next hundred years holds for Scattergood & Johnson Ltd no one can say – though it's a fair bet that this will continue in a very positive way.

Berwin & Berwin - Quality clothing for more than a century

The Berwin & Berwin's story goes back as far as 1885. Four generations on, this family run business continues to build not only its reputation but also the scale of its operations.

Now one of Europe's largest suit producers, with sites in Hungary and China, and offices in London, Leeds, and Budapest – the company is a key player in the manufacture and distribution of men's and women's tailored garments to the UK, European and other markets. Today Berwin & Berwin produces more than 20,000 suits each week.

Berwin & Berwin is one of the biggest suppliers to High Street chain NEXT, as well as Austin Reed, Moss Bros and Suits You. The firm operates Men's Suit Concessions in every House Of Fraser store in the UK.

Above: Founder Barnett Berwin.
Right: Ted Berwin.

In January 2006 Berwin Woman was launched and is now supplying many leading High Street retailers.

The Company also makes suits as well as offering casualwear under the Berwin & Berwin, Daniel Hechter, Chester by Chester Barrie and Ben Sherman labels.

Barnett Berlyn, a craftsman tailor from Bobruisk, a village in Belarus, Russia, had begun work there in 1885, before moving with his family to Leeds. His three sons, Louis, Ted and Jack, turned the firm into a genuine family business.

The family set up home in Trafalgar Street, part of the area known as Leylands. Barnett, his wife Sarah, their three sons and, daughters, Betsy, Leah and Joan later moved to Coburg Street, an area later to be occupied by the Merrion Centre.

Barnett became a foreman for John Barron the large suit manufacturer, who employed many Jewish immigrants in the city, but by 1920 he had set up on his own. Joined by Louis and working from Coburg Street this was the beginning of the business. Ted joined his father and brother taking on the role of salesman, making his first call to Barrow in Furness where he persuaded a retailer to give the fledgling firm some work.

Soon the business was making suits, jackets and, in particular, raincoats. Larger premises in Bridge Street

soon became necessary to accommodate the extra trade.

In the 1930s the business continued to prosper and additional premises were acquired in St Peter's Building opposite what would become the bus station.

Yet not everything went well. A large

Louis' son, Malcolm Berwin, joined the business in 1951 after National Service and graduation from Leeds University. He injected modern management and production techniques and succeeded in pushing the company back over the infamous 'North/South divide'.

The 1960s saw Berwin & Berwin continue to grow, employing 300 staff by the middle of the decade. Louis Berwin died in 1964 and Malcolm became a director.

By the end of the decade increased production demanded new premises: the three small factories were combined into one modern unit at Roseville Rd, Leeds in 1971 (still the headquarters of Berwin & Berwin today). The company's current MD, Malcolm's son Simon Berwin, joined in 1973.

The company trebled in size in the mid 1990s yet within a few short years its entire profile would change beyond recognition.

In order to meet world wide competition, the Company ended production in the UK in 2002 and moved its manufacturing operations to Hungary where it now employs around 1,000 people.

In September 2006 the business opened one of the biggest and most up to date suit factories in the world; an 18,000 sq metre factory in the Shandong Province of North East China in association with a Chinese conglomerate, Nanshan. The new Chinese venture will employ 1,300, working under ideal conditions.

London customer went into liquidation leaving a considerable amount owing. The brothers were so hurt that they vowed never to trade with a London-based company again – a policy which remained in force until the 1960s.

Before the business became a limited company in 1933 the family name was changed to Berwin in response to the prejudice that the name Berlyn had attracted as result of the first world war. By 1935 the company had grown sufficiently to relocate from its two separate sites to a larger factory in Roseville Road. Sadly Barnett Berwin died before he could see its completion.

During the second world war the firm was selected to make high-specification uniforms for US army officers.

The post war years saw the business prosper again. A new factory was acquired at Westland Road off Dewsbury Road solely for the production of raincoats.

Top left: Machinists at work.
Above left: Cloth cutting.
Below: The company's new 18,00 sq metre factory in China.

Yorkshire Fittings -
More than a century of innovation

Yorkshire Fittings Ltd of Leeds has been working with copper and its alloys since Queen Victoria's reign. From its base in Stourton it has developed its range of fittings and valves to such a degree that they are now recognised by the industry as amongst the best-engineered products of their kind in the world.

The first industrial use of the Stourton site dates to 1888 when Elmore's Depositing Co. made copper tubes there. In the early 1880s however the site had been a racecourse and the venue for the St Leger.

Elmore's Depositing Co. became the Yorkshire Copper Works in 1909 producing high quality condensing tubing.

The outbreak of the First World War in 1914 saw a break in tube production when the company facilities were requisitioned to manufacture munitions. The Great War also saw an influx of women workers brought in to carry out the often hard physical work in place of husbands, sons and brothers away in the fighting forces.

By the 1920s however normal production was resumed.

During the 1930s the country experienced a terrible economic depression, but the company was able to expand due to the inter-war house building programme.

Following the introduction in 1934 of the still-famous Yorkshire integral solder ring fitting the business

boomed. In 1958 the company merged with ICI's Metals Division and become YIM - Yorkshire Imperial Metals.

Eventually YIM was incorporated into the Building Products Group of IMI plc and later took on the name IMI Yorkshire Fittings Ltd.

Today Yorkshire Fittings is part of Aalberts Industries, an international industrial group of companies. Collaboration with Aalberts Industries sister companies has resulted in the significant expansion of the company's product portfolio to include plumbing and heating system solutions and heat-free fittings systems. Indeed, Yorkshire Fittings is now a leading manufacturer of fittings and valves for the plumbing, heating, ventilating and air conditioning industries.

The famous Yorkshire integral solder ring fitting is still manufactured exclusively at the Leeds site, which is also the base for extensive research and development into new jointing techniques. More than a century of accumulated experience of working with copper to develop solutions for pipework system designers and installers has given Yorkshire Fittings the ability to manufacture the highest quality products for industrial and domestic users throughout the world.

Top right: The Rt Hon Edward Heath inspects an abstract form of tubes when visiting Yorkshire Fittings in 1963.
Left: The latest product innovation-Tectite Sprint push-fit fittings.

The City Varieties - A star is born

In 1894 a new name, The City Varieties Music Hall, appeared in Leeds. Today it is listed in the Guinness Book of Records for being Britain's longest running music hall.

The history of this fascinating venue however spans more than two centuries. The White Swan was a coaching inn built about 1750. A century later it was taken over by a publican named Charles Thornton. He saw how popular music hall shows were and decided to rebuild the White Swan singing room. He named it Thornton's New Music Hall and Fashionable Lounge: the opening night was 7th June 1865. In March 1897 a group of clog dancers were engaged. They were Eight Lancashire Lads, one of whom was Charlie Chaplin: the City Varieties is the last surviving theatre in Britain where Chaplin once tread the boards. Chaplin, Lily Langtrey, Harry Houdini, Charles Lawton and nearly all the great performers of the age would appear there.

In 1913 the building was sold to the Palace Theatre Company and subsequently passed through a number of owners until in 1947 it was bought by Harry Joseph, managing director of British Union Varieties Ltd.In 1953 the music hall was used for the pilot programme of a new music hall series the Good Old Days, produced and directed by Barney Colehan for BBC Television.

In 1960 The City Varieties was scheduled as a building of special architectural and historical interest. Upon the death of their father in 1962, control passed to Michael and Stanley Joseph. 1968 saw the return, after 20 years of pantomime productions. The final programme of BBC TV's series Good Old Days came in 1983. The building was sold to the Leeds Grand Theatre & Opera House Ltd in 1987. The following year saw the re-launch of the Good Old Days as a stage show under the continuing direction of Barney Colehan until death in 1991.

During the 1990s major repairs and refurbishment ensured that this remarkable theatre will remain in a jewel Leeds' civic crown for many more years to come.Today the theatre rightly enjoys both national and international acclaim as a star in its own right.

Top: *The Good Old Days produced and directed by Barney Colehan for BBC Television.* ***Left:*** *The City Varieties Music Hall, 2006.*

Grand Theatre - A Grand performance

Leeds Grand Theatre and Opera House has captivated audiences for more than a century with entertainment ranging from ballet to revue, through comedy and drama to musicals and pantomime.

Since its opening in 1878 all the great names of theatre have trodden the boards at the Grand: Ellen Terry, Lily Langtry, Sarah Bernhardt, Sir Laurence Olivier, Dame Sybil Thorndike and Ivor Novello. In more recent times the theatre has witnessed performances by Norman Wisdom, Britt Ekland, David Soul, Russ Abbot, Liz Dawn, Gerry & the Pacemakers and a galaxy of other stars.

Built by architect George Corson, the theatre is a mixture of styles with a Gothic façade that belies the interior splendour. With a seating capacity of 1,450, the Grand is the largest theatre in Leeds: it has a classic proscenium arch with stalls, dress circle, balconies and boxes. The Grand has become synonymous with all that is best in the performing arts. For more than a quarter of a century the theatre has been home to Opera North, one of Britain's best-loved and most highly respected opera companies, and is the performing home of Northern Ballet Theatre. The theatre frequently stages hit West End and Broadway musicals and continues to attract the biggest names in show business.

In 2006 Phase I of a £31.5 million refurbishment of the Grand Theatre was completed. A state-of-the-art computerised flying system was installed and a lorry lift which facilitates the movement of larger, more complex sets enabling world class productions to appear in the future.

The stalls area has been completely re-raked to provide more legroom and improved sight lines. Wider seats using revolutionary new body contour foam that moulds to the person have been fitted in all areas. An improved air-conditioning system provides audiences with an ambient temperature all year round, and a deeper, enlarged orchestra pit significantly improves acoustics. A new front of house lift provides access to all seating levels, whilst wheelchair access has been significantly enhanced. Today Leeds Grand Theatre and Opera House is recognised as a centre of excellence for entertainment and culture not only in the North of England but also as one of the most popular theatres in the country.

Above: *An interior view of the refurbished auditorium.*
Below: *An artist's impression of the Grand Theatre after phases I and II of the refurbishment.*

Opera North - The sound of Leeds

© Stephen Vaughan

Since 1978 Opera North has been England's national opera company in the North proudly based in Leeds. It is one of Europe's leadings arts organisations and produces work of the highest quality. Its newly created Opera Centre has opened up new opportunities to bring the magic of music and opera into the lives of future generations.

Opera North tours not only throughout the North of England and to London, but also to opera houses on the continent in cities such as Prague and Barcelona, and performs at major international festivals including Edinburgh and Ravenna.

An innovative approach to programming and performance style has been widely acknowledged through a number of prestigious awards, including no fewer than four for its Eight Little Greats season in 2004 and the Royal Philharmonic Society Opera and Music Theatre Awards 2005.

From its home at Leeds Grand Theatre, the Company actively challenges conventional perceptions of opera, breathing new life into the classics. The Company is also a strong advocate of lesser- known works and a champion of musical theatre.

Opera North collaborates with artists and companies working in a variety of media, including film and visual art. Its versatile Chorus and Orchestra also perform independently. The Orchestra runs the concert series at Huddersfield and Dewsbury Town Halls and regularly appears in the Leeds International Concert Series.

Education is a vital part of the work of the Company. Opera North Education is one of the leading arts education departments in the country and around 9,000 young people come into contact with the department every year. The team delivers a range of workshops and creative projects, encouraging young people and communities to explore the art form of opera.

Opera North is proud of its northern roots and provides a valuable resource for the cultural life of the region and for the development of young talent. The work of Opera North is made possible by direct support of Arts Council England, local authorities led by a close and sustained relationship with Leeds City Council, sponsorship from the private sector, the Friends of Opera North and the Opera North Fund, and not least its paying audiences which assist Opera North to continue its award-winning programmes.

Top left: *La Vida Breve, part of the award-winning Eight Little Greats festival.* ***Below:*** *Opera North's Rigoletto which opened the newly refurbished Leeds Grand Theatre.*

© Stephen Vaughan

ACKNOWLEDGMENTS

The publishers would like to thank

West Yorkshire Archive Service

Leeds City Libraries Local Studies Library

Andrew Mitchell

Steve Ainsworth

True North Books Ltd - Book List

Memories of Accrington - 1 903204 05 4

Memories of Barnet - 1 903204 16 X

Memories of Barnsley - 1 900463 11 3

More Memories of Barnsley - 1 903 204 79 8

Golden Years of Barnsley -1 900463 87 3

Memories of Basingstoke - 1 903204 26 7

Memories of Bedford - 1 900463 83 0

More Memories of Bedford - 1 903204 33 X

Golden Years of Birmingham - 1 900463 04 0

Birmingham Memories - 1 903204 45 3

More Birmingham Memories - 1 903204 80 1

Memories of Blackburn - 1 900463 40 7

More Memories of Blackburn - 1 900463 96 2

Memories of Blackpool - 1 900463 21 0

Memories of Bolton - 1 900463 45 8

More Memories of Bolton - 1 900463 13 X

Bolton Memories - 1 903204 37 2

Memories of Bournemouth -1 900463 44 X

Memories of Bradford - 1 900463 00 8

More Memories of Bradford - 1 900463 16 4

More Memories of Bradford II - 1 900463 63 6

Bradford Memories - 1 903204 47 X

Bradford City Memories - 1 900463 57 1

Memories of Bristol - 1 900463 78 4

More Memories of Bristol - 1 903204 43 7

Memories of Bromley - 1 903204 21 6

Memories of Burnley - 1 900463 95 4

Golden Years of Burnley - 1 900463 67 9

Memories of Bury - 1 900463 90 3

More Memories of Bury - 1 903 204 78 X

Memories of Cambridge - 1 900463 88 1

Memories of Cardiff - 1 900463 14 8

More Memories of Cardiff - 1 903204 73 9

Memories of Carlisle - 1 900463 38 5

Memories of Chelmsford - 1 903204 29 1

Memories of Cheltenham - 1 903204 17 8

Memories of Chester - 1 900463 46 6

More Memories of Chester -1 903204 02 X

Chester Memories - 1 903204 83 6

Memories of Chesterfield -1 900463 61 X

More Memories of Chesterfield - 1 903204 28 3

Memories of Colchester - 1 900463 74 1

Nostalgic Coventry - 1 900463 58 X

Coventry Memories - 1 903204 38 0

Memories of Croydon - 1 900463 19 9

More Memories of Croydon - 1 903204 35 6

Golden Years of Darlington - 1 900463 72 5

Nostalgic Darlington - 1 900463 31 8

Darlington Memories - 1 903204 46 1

Memories of Derby - 1 900463 37 7

More Memories of Derby - 1 903204 20 8

Memories of Dewsbury & Batley - 1 900463 80 6

Memories of Doncaster - 1 900463 36 9

More Memories of Doncaster - 1 903204 75 5

Nostalgic Dudley - 1 900463 03 2

Golden Years of Dudley - 1 903204 60 7

Memories of Edinburgh - 1 900463 33 4

More memories of Edinburgh - 1903204 72 0

Memories of Enfield - 1 903204 14 3

Memories of Exeter - 1 900463 94 6

Memories of Glasgow - 1 900463 68 7

More Memories of Glasgow - 1 903204 44 5

Memories of Gloucester - 1 903204 04 6

Memories of Grimsby - 1 900463 97 0

More Memories of Grimsby - 1 903204 36 4

Memories of Guildford - 1 903204 22 4

Memories of Halifax - 1 900463 05 9

More Memories of Halifax - 1 900463 06 7

Golden Years of Halifax - 1 900463 62 8

Nostalgic Halifax - 1 903204 30 5

Memories of Harrogate - 1 903204 01 1

Memories of Hartlepool - 1 900463 42 3

Memories of High Wycombe - 1 900463 84 9

Memories of Huddersfield - 1 900463 15 6

More Memories of Huddersfield - 1 900463 26 1

Golden Years of Huddersfield - 1 900463 77 6

Nostalgic Huddersfield - 1 903204 19 4

Huddersfield Memories - 1903204 86 0

Huddersfield Town FC - 1 900463 51 2

Memories of Hull - 1 900463 86 5

More Memories of Hull - 1 903204 06 2

Hull Memories - 1 903204 70 4

True North Books Ltd - Book List

Memories of Keighley - 1 900463 01 6

Golden Years of Keighley - 1 900463 92 X

Memories of Kingston - 1 903204 24 0

Memories of Leeds - 1 900463 75 X

More Memories of Leeds - 1 900463 12 1

Golden Years of Leeds - 1 903204 07 0

Memories of Leicester - 1 900463 08 3

Leeds Memories - 1 903204 62 3

More Leeds Memories - 1 903204 90 9

More Memories of Leicester - 1 903204 08 9

Memories of Leigh - 1 903204 27 5

Memories of Lincoln - 1 900463 43 1

Memories of Liverpool - 1 900463 07 5

More Memories of Liverpool - 1 903204 09 7

Liverpool Memories - 1 903204 53 4

More Liverpool Memories - 1 903204 88 7

Memories of Luton - 1 900463 93 8

Memories of Macclesfield - 1 900463 28 8

Memories of Manchester - 1 900463 27 X

More Memories of Manchester - 1 903204 03 8

Manchester Memories - 1 903204 54 2

More Manchester Memories - 1 903204 89 5

Memories of Middlesbrough - 1 900463 56 3

More Memories of Middlesbrough - 1 903204 42 9

Memories of Newbury - 1 900463 79 2

Memories of Newcastle - 1 900463 81 4

More Memories of Newcastle - 1 903204 10 0

Newcastle Memories - 1.903204 71 2

Memories of Newport - 1 900463 59 8

Memories of Northampton - 1 900463 48 2

More Memories of Northampton - 1 903204 34 8

Memories of Norwich - 1 900463 73 3

Memories of Nottingham - 1 900463 91 1

More Memories of Nottingham - 1 903204 11 9

Nottingham Memories - 1 903204 63 1

Bygone Oldham - 1 900463 25 3

Memories of Oldham - 1 900463 76 8

More Memories of Oldham - 1 903204 84 4

Memories of Oxford - 1 900463 54 7

Memories of Peterborough - 1 900463 98 9

Golden Years of Poole - 1 900463 69 5

Memories of Portsmouth - 1 900463 39 3

More Memories of Portsmouth - 1 903204 51 8

Nostalgic Preston - 1 900463 50 4

More Memories of Preston - 1 900463 17 2

Preston Memories - 1 903204 41 0

Memories of Reading - 1 900463 49 0

Memories of Rochdale - 1 900463 60 1

More Memories of Reading - 1 903204 39 9

More Memories of Rochdale - 1 900463 22 9

Memories of Romford - 1 903204 40 2

Memories of Rotherham- 1903204 77 1

Memories of St Albans - 1 903204 23 2

Memories of St Helens - 1 900463 52 0

Memories of Sheffield - 1 900463 20 2

More Memories of Sheffield - 1 900463 32 6

Golden Years of Sheffield - 1 903204 13 5

Memories of Slough - 1 900 463 29 6

Golden Years of Solihull - 1 903204 55 0

Memories of Southampton - 1 900463 34 2

More Memories of Southampton - 1 903204 49 6

Memories of Stockport - 1 900463 55 5

More Memories of Stockport - 1 903204 18 6

Stockport Memories - 1 903204 87 9

Memories of Stockton - 1 900463 41 5

Memories of Stoke-on-Trent - 1 900463 47 4

More Memories of Stoke-on-Trent - 1 903204 12 7

Memories of Stourbridge - 1903204 31 3

Memories of Sunderland - 1 900463 71 7

More Memories of Sunderland - 1 903204 48 8

Memories of Swindon - 1 903204 00 3

Memories of Uxbridge - 1 900463 64 4

Memories of Wakefield - 1 900463 65 2

More Memories of Wakefield - 1 900463 89 X

Nostalgic Walsall - 1 900463 18 0

Golden Years of Walsall - 1 903204 56 9

More Memories of Warrington - 1 900463 02 4

Warrington Memories - 1 903204 85 2

Memories of Watford - 1 900463 24 5

Golden Years of West Bromwich - 1 900463 99 7

Memories of Wigan - 1 900463 85 7

Golden Years of Wigan - 1 900463 82 2

More Memories of Wigan - 1 903204 82 8

Nostalgic Wirral - 1 903204 15 1

Wirral Memories - 1 903204 747

Memories of Woking - 1 903204 32 1

Nostalgic Wolverhampton - 1 900463 53 9

Wolverhampton Memories - 1 903204 50 X

Memories of Worcester - 1 903204 25 9

Memories of Wrexham - 1 900463 23 7

Memories of York - 1 900463 66 0